253 Jac 14702

Jackso
Pastor
and en

PASTORPRENEUR

Pastors and
Entrepreneurs
Answer the Call

PASTORPRENEUR

Dr. John Jackson

Foreword by John Maxwell

Published in the United States by Baxter Press, Friendswood, Texas.
Front cover design by Bob Contreras, Direct Effect Marketing, LLC.
Dust jacket layout by John Gilmore, Gilmore Marketing.
Formatted by Anne McLaughlin, Blue Lake Design, Dickinson, Texas.

ISBN: 1-888237-45-7

The version of the Bible used in this book is the New International Version.

Dedication

This book is dedicated to the pastors, church leaders, and business leaders upon whose shoulders I stand. These pastors and leaders motivated their churches to embrace the creative, the impossible, or the unusual in order to impact their culture. The message of the gospel will never change . . . the methods of reaching the culture with the gospel message must always change so we are as effective as possible!

"And I will not be won by weaklings, subtle and suave
    and mild,
But by men with the hearts of Vikings and the simple faith
    of a child,
Desperate, strong, and resistless, unthrottled by fear or defeat,
Them will I gild with my treasure, them will I glut with
    my meat."

—From "Law of the Yukon," by Robert W. Service

Table of Contents

Acknowledgments

I want to thank my brother Gene Jackson for his radical commitment to the ministry of the local church and for his leadership of Kingdom Ventures into "uncharted territory" in this new millennium.

The people of Carson Valley Christian Center deserve high praise for their unfailing commitment to see lives change through dynamic encounters with Jesus Christ. My teammates in leadership and staff colleagues in ministry at Carson Valley Christian Center are always supportive and to them I owe a huge debt of gratitude.

Pat Springle of Baxter Press made this work possible. (Pat, I'm still reading all the books we talked about during this process!)

My children, Jennifer, Dena, Rachel, Joshua, and Harrison are the delight of my life.

My wife Pamela is the foundation of hope and stability for our home, and I will never be able to adequately express my gratitude to her.

Finally, I wish to acknowledge the unbelievable work of grace that Jesus Christ is doing in my life . . . I can't wait to see what God makes of me over time and all eternity!

Foreword

*S*trategic thinking can change your life. In fact, in my book, *Thinking for a Change* (Warner Business Books), I write that "strategic thinking simplifies the difficult and prepares you for an uncertain tomorrow." And there is no other place on earth where strategic thinking is more needed and perhaps less applied than the local church. It is a place that faces some of life's most difficult challenges, often filled with people facing uncertain tomorrows.

Pastors across the land are overwhelmed, discouraged, and frustrated. But if they would embrace strategic thinking it would better prepare them for the uncertainties that lie ahead. It would allow them to be more effective in their ministry. Strategic thinking is a different way of thinking. It doesn't always come naturally. And although it might be frightening for some to step out into the unknown, in my experience such a step is worth the risk.

My love for strategic thinking is a big part of the reason I'm recommending, *PastorPreneur: Pastors and Entrepreneurs Answer the Call*. In this book, my friend, John Jackson, shares with passion the philosophy of ministry he's developed at one of the emerging churches in the American West, Carson Valley Christian Center. John planted the church in 1998 and has seen it grow to a thriving congregation of over 2,000 in less than five years.

John's a strategic thinker. He's a visionary. But he knows that reaching others for Christ is not his vision alone. In the past few years he's also become a great empowerer to others in the ministry. John believes in partnerships and alliances, and he loves working with others. He's not been afraid to ask others to take the journey with him. The result? Thousands are taking that journey today that weren't just a half decade ago. Carson Valley Christian Center is succeeding due to a focused vision coupled with strategic thinking.

If you're thinking your way through developing a new church or being an agent for change in your present ministry, *PastorPreneur* is worth reading. John Jackson knows what he's talking about because he's lived it. For John and the people at Carson Valley Christian Center, changed thinking has been worth the risk. I know it will be for you too!

John C. Maxwell
Founder – The INJOY Group

Introduction

In my 23 years of ministry, God has given me enough success to keep me enthusiastic and enough failure to keep me dependent on him. This book distills the lessons I've learned from all my experiences, from the sublime to the ridiculous. I'm excited to be able to share these lessons with you.

From my discussions with pastors, church leaders, and Christian business leaders, I realize there are two types of people who may pick up a book like this. One type is reflective and wants to understand the *whys* as much as the *whats* and *hows* of any ministry strategy. Another type is the hard charging, go-for-it person who is eager to take action. Their attitude is: "Just point the way. I'm ready to go!" This book is written for both types of people.

Most church leaders and Christian business people will benefit from the first four chapters' description of our calling to take bold risks for Christ's sake. These chapters provide the biblical foundations for the strategies that follow, and they give depth and meaning to our call to boldness. I recommend that you take the time to read these chapters carefully to prepare your mind and heart for the chapters on strategies. But if you are a can-do, no-nonsense, action-oriented person, you may want to read the first chapter and then move directly to the five strategies.

The leadership team at our church benefits greatly from our discussions of ministry philosophy and strategies. I hope you and the leadership team at your church will use this book as a springboard for great interaction, and I trust God will use your discussions to propel you to dare to dream big dreams that will honor him. If every church had an entrepreneurial pastor and entrepreneurial leaders growing and learning together, we'd see God-sized dreams coming to pass!

chapter 1

God's Call to Bold Action

"The wicked man flees though no one pursues, but the righteous are as bold as a lion"
(Prov 28:1).

Business as usual just won't cut it anymore. The church has been a bedrock foundation of Western society for hundreds of years, but today the church is standing on the edge of irrelevance. We need a fresh, bold, articulate vision for ministry. Incremental change and small refinements in current ministry practices are of only limited value in making the church a dynamic force for good.

In his insightful book, *Dancing with the Dinosaurs*, William Easum wrote, "If churches only improve what they have been doing, they will die. Bureaucracies and traditional practices are the major cause of the decline of most denominations in North America."[1] George Barna goes one step further when he says, "Let's cut to the chase. After nearly two decades of studying Christian churches in America, I'm convinced that the typical church as we know it today has a rapidly expiring shelf life."[2]

As I have shared my vision for change with a number of pastors, some have called this "an entrepreneurial strategy for churches." It combines the aggressive goals of business

---

1   William Easum, *Dancing with Dinosaurs,* p. 13-14, www.easumbandy.com.
2   George Barna, *The Second Coming of the Church,* (Word Publishing, Nashville, Tennessee, 2001), p. 1.

A pastorpreneur is an innovative Christian leader, a creative dreamer who is willing to take great risks in church ministry with the hope of great gain for Christ and his kingdom.

with God's heart for people. I later merged these ideas and coined the term *pastorpreneur*. A pastorpreneur is an innovative Christian leader (pastor, lay leader or Christian business person), a creative dreamer who is willing to take great risks in church ministry with the hope of great gain for Christ and his kingdom. Like any good entrepreneur, this kind of leader isn't wild-eyed and foolish. He assesses goals, opportunities, and risks very carefully, but he is willing to attempt great things for God. His path is checkered with successes and defeats, but his successes touch many more people than if he had chosen to play it safe. And he learns from his failures so even they are stepping-stones to future gains.

In this book, I want to challenge pastors and church leaders to take bold steps, to dream big dreams, to take risks to accomplish more for God's glory than they ever dreamed possible. These leaders can implement the five strategies outlined in these pages. But also, I want to invite a host of Christians in the business community to connect with God's heart and these strategies at particular points, such as becoming partners with their churches to create faith-building, community-wide events that touch thousands of lives. I believe there are men and women in every church who long for their lives to count for Christ. They only need the opportunity to use their skills and resources for God.

Throughout church history, God has called men and women to galvanize the church's vision at crucial times and to originate bold new strategies that made a difference. The Apostle Paul's missionary journeys established churches throughout the Roman world. He boldly proclaimed the gospel of Christ to Romans and barbarians. Nothing could stop him. He was a revolutionary when he was free and when he was in prison, when he was popular and when he was despised. His passion for Christ energized his generation and his example of zeal and strategy for the cause of Christ continues to influence leaders today. In a summary of his passion for taking the gospel to every person in the world, he wrote:

"Though I am free and belong to no man, I make myself a slave to everyone, to win as many as possible. To the Jews I became a Jew, to win the Jews . . . . To the weak I became weak, to win the weak. I have become all things to all men so that by all possible means I might save some. I do all this for the sake of the gospel, that I may share in its blessings" (I Cor 9:19-23).

Paul didn't feel bound to do the same things in the same ways they had been done before. The church was brand new, and his strategy was directed by God to meet the complex needs of establishing the church. Paul is not alone in his pioneer spirit. In the great century of missions, people like William Carey, Adoniram Judson, and Hudson Taylor charted new courses to win the world for Christ. John Mott and the Student Volunteer Movement responded to the world's needs and reached millions of people who had never heard the name of Jesus. In recent years, churches like Willow Creek Community Church and Saddleback Community Church have broken the mold of church strategy. They began with only God's clear call, and they have become examples of vision and activism that directly and indirectly touch millions of lives. All of these pioneers remind me of the proverb: "The wicked man flees though no one pursues, but the righteous are as bold as a lion" (Prov 28:1).

Seeing the success of other's bold strategies, we are left with the questions: Are we content to remain comfortable doing ministry the way we have always done it, with some positive but limited results, knowing in our hearts that we aren't making much of a dent in our culture? Or will we take the risk of boldly trusting God for a fresh vision, powerful strategies, and incredible results? I believe that a fresh, Spirit-led burst of entrepreneurial activity will lead the church to greater impact than ever before.

Go for the Gold

Elisabeth Elliott has written eloquently of her husband's preparation for the mission field. Jim was a young lion who compared his commitment to Christ and the Great Commission to miners who went to the frozen Yukon a century ago. Both expected great risks and hardships, although the difficulties of the journey paled in comparison to the promise of rich rewards. The miners had been after tangible but temporal gold, while Elliott sought "spiritual" gold, silver, and precious stones that will never pass away (1 Cor 3:12). In those days of steeling himself to face the risks that lay ahead (dangers that proved to be very real indeed), Jim copied part of "The Law of the Yukon," a poem by Robert W. Service, in his journal. Elisabeth Elliott included the passage in her book, *The Path of Loneliness.*[3] It reads:

> "Send not your foolish and feeble; send me your
> strong and your sane,
> Strong for the red-rage of battle, sane for I harry
> them sore.
> Send me men girt for the combat, men who are grit
> to the core. . . .

3   Elisabeth Elliott, *The Path of Loneliness,* (Servant Publications, Grand Rapids, Michigan, 2001), pp. 105-106.

And I wait for the men who will win me—and I will
    not be won in a day,
And I will not be won by weaklings, subtle and suave
    and mild,
But by men with the hearts of Vikings and the sim-
    ple faith of a child,
Desperate, strong, and resistless, unthrottled by fear
    or defeat,
Them will I gild with my treasure, them will I glut
    with my meat."

This poem touched Jim Elliott's deep-est longings to be strong in the cause of Christ, to have the boldness of a lion and the faith of a child in taking the gospel to the world. The promise of gold was worth any sacrifice to the miners who braved the incredibly difficult journey over parts of Canada and Alaska to get to the goldfields. That expectation instilled them with passion, hope, and courage.

That expectation instilled them with passion, hope, and courage.

As church leaders today, what are the promises and expectations that drive us? These things are not always clear for most of us. It is easy for us to be comfortable and rea-sonably successful doing what we've always done before. Many church leaders are satisfied with small changes, tweak-ing systems, and a little growth. Some of us, however, know there's more. We're convinced that now is the time for a new direction. Now is the time for boldness.

God's promise to us is even more compelling than the promise of Yukon gold: *It is the promise of being used by the God of the universe in his holy cause to rescue men and women from darkness so they can be transferred into his kingdom.* And the promise to each of us is that if we follow God's heart and path, in the end we will hear those wonderful words, "Well done, good and faithful servant. Enter into the joy of your Master." That reward will be worth far more than gold.

Jim Elliott's clear perception of unseen treasure and his tenacity to take any risks to accomplish God's purpose is the theme throughout this book. And because he was so inspired by the miner metaphor to illustrate our commitment to Christ and his cause, we will refer to it often.

Snapshots

Let's take a look at some of today's bold and entrepreneurial pioneers. At Westwinds Community Church in Michigan, pastor Ron Martoia and his congregation are using drama, technology, and strong relational connections to invite previously unchurched people to respond to Christ. They are helping the church speak the language of the culture instead of demanding that the culture speak the language of the church. Martoia describes this bold strategy in his book, *Morph!* (Published by Group Publishing). At a turning point a few years ago, he had to choose between following the normal, accepted patterns of ministry that offered incremental growth or taking the risk to do something new. He didn't know if the unbelievers in his community would respond positively, and he didn't know if his own people would run him out of town on a rail, but he was willing to trust God for great things. He risked failure, ridicule, and irrelevance in his own church. He risked being labeled as a rebel—and if his experiment didn't work, a *failed* rebel—and possibly never finding another church that would hire him.

When Ed Young put a fitness center, basketball court, and bowling alleys in Second Baptist Church in Houston, many people criticized him for being worldly. But Young understood his community, and he believed God wanted his church to be a haven for families as well as an outreach to the lost. As a result, the sports emphasis attracted people to his church who would never have come first to a sanctuary, yet who felt completely comfortable coming to the church to work out. Most of them made new friends there, and many of them trusted Christ as their Savior. This strategy is fairly common today, but it was radical 30 years ago when Ed Young took this bold step.

Kirby John Caldwell became the pastor of Windsor Village United Methodist Church in Houston, Texas, an old church of about 60 people that was seeing, at best, slow growth. After God gave him a fresh vision for ministry, he established nine nonprofit corporations to address problems of subpar housing, education, and vocational skills. These corporations helped improve the living conditions for people in the community as the church was introducing them to Christ, which proved to be a powerful synergy of efforts.

With any target audience, Christian leaders must learn to think outside the box. Evangelicals may feel very comfortable blending social activism with preaching the gospel. We are happy to volunteer at a homeless shelter and give groceries to the food bank to provide a platform for the message of Christ. But the middle and upper classes also have needs that can be creatively addressed.

With any target audience, Christian leaders must learn to think outside the box.

Robert Schuller has long been a pioneer in reaching out to people. His simple but powerful philosophy is: "Find a need and fill it. Find a hurt and heal it." That perspective will always lead a church to relevance in its community.

In Granite Bay, California, Ray Johnston established Bayside Covenant Church in a community holding the perception that only women and weak men are interested in

Jesus Christ. Spirituality, they believed, is only "for those who can't cut it in life. " Before going to Granite Bay, Ray had ministered to teenagers all across the country. He positioned his new ministry to speak powerfully to the hopes and fears of "up and outers," especially in their relationships with their teenage children. He risks speaking of the relevance of Christ to those who saw no relevance, and in fact, who have long held very negative attitudes toward the message of Christ and the church.

During our first year at Carson Valley Christian Center, a man came up to me during one of our training events. He said, "I've listened to you, and I've watched what you're doing here. It doesn't look like you have a 'Plan B' if your strategy to reach the community fails."

I told him, "You're exactly right. We're completely committed to our vision, sink or swim." That man was a shrewd observer. From the beginning, we determined to trust God for great things. We didn't think small, we didn't *believe* small, and we didn't *behave* small. I went to meetings of the Chamber of Commerce and told them our dream for our church to have a significant impact on this community. The risk was that I'd be laughed out of town after a couple of years if we didn't grow. This clear and singular vision for our church wasn't developed in a vacuum. God brought together a wonderful group of people who sacrificed time, money, and energy to invest their lives in reaching this area of Nevada for Christ. We all risked a lot.

Bold leaders often face risks in the area of finances. In the first century, religious leaders expected to be funded by those who followed their teaching. Certainly, Paul could have instructed the churches to provide for him. They often did so voluntarily, but not always. Paul was so committed to the vision of reaching the world for Christ that he used any and every means to keep himself on the cutting edge. If funding was available from the churches, he accepted it. If not, he gladly made tents to fund his ministry. He never complained because he had "learned the secret of being content" as he passionately followed Christ and took the gospel to the world. His example is one we can learn from today.

From Him, by Him, for Him

The vision of what God can do through us is not one we concoct on our own. It is given to each believer by God, it is accomplished by his power, and we do it for his glory. Author Os Guinness says that the calling of God is not just for pastors. As each of us is gripped with the love and power of our Lord, we gladly give up everything to follow him and accomplish his purposes. "Calling," wrote Guinness, "is the truth that God calls us to himself so decisively that everything we are, everything we do, and everything we have is invested with a special devotion and dynamism lived out as a response to his summons and service."[4]

Those who are gripped by big goals understand that when God is the source of those goals, he provides wisdom and strength to fulfill them. And those who are motivated by seeing people's hearts changed realize that we have the unspeakable privilege of being God's partners in touching others' lives. Our dream of being used by God comes from him, our desire is purified and directed by him, and its fulfillment is for his honor because he deserves our glad obedience and praise.

Far too often, people (even church leaders) simply try to squeeze Christ into their busy lives, expecting him to accomplish the goals they have already set for themselves.

> *As each of us is gripped with the love and power of our Lord, we gladly give up everything to follow him and accomplish his purposes.*

---

4   Os Guinness, *The Call*, (Nashville: Word Publishing, 1998), p. 4.

Christ is worthy of much more than that. He is the Lord, the Sovereign over all of creation, the Alpha and the Omega, the Word, and the Lamb of God who takes away the sins of the world.

During his earthly ministry, Jesus' call to his disciples was simple: "Follow me." That calling was absolute, complete, and compelling to the Twelve. It is no less for us today. As Guinness clearly stated, God's calling forms the basis of our identity so that everything we are and everything we do has far deeper meaning because every thought, word, and deed can honor the One who has called us to be his. He deserves our very best, and that very best means that we are willing to sacrifice all for him and risk all for him. We are no longer content to play it safe. No, we grow bold and want the reputation of his goodness and greatness to spread to every part of our communities and our world. He deserves nothing less than that.

My Own Background

I was born and raised in a pastor's home. When I was a child, some people prayed for me, patted my head, and told me that I was going to be a pastor just like my Dad. When I heard those words, I gritted my teeth and said under my breath, "Not if I can help it!" At the time, my dream, goal, and passion was to become a professional baseball player. In high school, I began thinking more deeply about God's calling in my life. I still wanted to play baseball, but even more, I wanted to do what God wanted me to do . . . with two exceptions. I was determined never to become a pastor or a missionary. I had grown up in a pastor's house, and I didn't want that lifestyle. And because missionaries wore grass skirts, lived in grass huts, and showed boring slide shows when they came back to America every 10 years or so, I didn't want to do that, either.

In spite of my rigid restrictions on God's will, he clearly called me to be a local church pastor. Even at a young age, I was convinced that God wanted me to go to college, then seminary, and then pastor a little church of 25 people or so in some remote town in the middle of nowhere. Like other pastors, my role would be to hatch, match, and dispatch (to see my congregation members through birth, marriage, and death). That, I was sure, was God's calling, so I became resigned to a rather mundane lifestyle for my future.

My role model, my Dad, could talk to a fence post and make it feel better, but planning and coordinating activities were not his leadership strengths. So when I became a youth pastor a few years later, I was surprised to discover that I had some administrative gifts. By the time I was 25 years old, I had earned a doctorate from a public university in Educational Administration with an emphasis in organizational behavior and leadership. Through a series of strange events, I became the pastor of a church of about 400 people who had been terribly wounded by betrayal and mistrust. My role was to provide healing and hope.

After a few years at that church, my denomination asked me to serve in a leadership role, so I became the youngest executive in the history of our denomination. I enjoyed using my leadership and administrative gifts, but denominational work is very political. Playing politics all day every day was a drain on me.

By the time I was 35, it could be said that God had called me, gifted me, and used me in some significant ways. But I lived with a secret: My life was too safe. In my heart, I knew I had never been willing to lay it all on the line for Jesus Christ, to trust God enough to risk personal failure. I'd

> *But I lived with a secret: My life was too safe.*

been successful at many things, but I'd never been willing to focus on one thing, one dream, "this one thing I do," as Paul defined his ministry. I'd been happy to use my God-given abilities at the level of an 8 or a 9 on a 10-point scale. That was very comfortable, but striving for a 10 demanded far more risk than I had ever experienced. For some time, I wrestled with this tension between comfort and risk.

At a retreat in the early months of 1996, I read an advance copy of Rick Warren's book, *The Purpose Driven Church*. The book contained part of his first sermon at Saddleback Community Church, which described his bold, sweeping vision for what the church would look like in 20 years. When I read it, I laughed out loud. *That's ridiculous!* I thought. *How could anybody have the audacity to stand up in front of 200 people (some of whom are family, so they had to be there) and tell them that in 20 years, the church would have 20,000 people on 50 acres in upscale Orange County, California? How arrogant!* I knew Saddleback and I knew Orange County—you just don't dream those kinds of dreams in that kind of place!

I went outside at the retreat center and walked in the snow. I felt like God had put a burning ember in my stomach. At that moment, God seemed to be saying to me, "Would you dare to dream big dreams for me?" That question presented a fork in the road for me. I instantly responded, "No!" I had a nice salary, a big office, and all the perks that come with being a denominational executive. I wasn't exactly happy in my role, but I assumed that eventually God would direct me back to a local church where I would be happier and more fulfilled. God's question was more than I bargained for. He was asking me to put my safety, my reputation, and my finances on the line to take a huge risk and trust him. Was I willing to put aside my salary,

> *"Would you dare to dream big dreams for me?"*

my office and perks, and my influence on 20,000 people in our denomination? Was I willing to leave safety behind and walk into the unknown?

In the hours after that question penetrated my heart that day in the snow, God began to clarify his direction for me. He was calling me to work with people who had given up on the traditional church but who hadn't given up on him. The more I thought about it, the more I realized this was unmistakably God's clear calling. During the next few months, my wife got excited about this dream. My brother, his wife, and two other couples were also very supportive. When I resigned my position at the denomination, we had very little money in savings and no money set aside for church planting, but God immediately began to confirm that we had done the right thing. In fact, some people on our Christmas card list committed $50,000, and two organizations gave another $200,000 to help us. This was an amazing confirmation of God working in our hearts, so we moved to Carson Valley, Nevada, to start a church.

Still, I was afraid that we would fail. My thoughts were haunted by images of a handful of people in a boring service five years after we started the church. But God reminded me that his calling is not about achievement; it's about faithfulness. My job is to respond to him. His job is to produce fruit in his way, in his timing, and for his glory.

The two words that have characterized my life since we began this new ministry are *focus* and *discipline*. God wanted me to focus on one thing, not fifty. What would God do if my heart and mind were focused like a laser beam on his purposes? And could I discipline my heart to want God's will and his ways more than the safety of business as usual?

Calling and Joy

When we think of sacrifice, we often imagine grim-faced resignation. But when we respond to God's calling, the safety we give up is replaced with the great joy of seeing God work in and through us. We are directed by the Way, inspired by the Truth, and empowered by the Life, and we discover the unspeakable privilege of representing him, of being his ambassadors to those around us. Peter described this privilege: "But you are a chosen people, a royal priesthood, a holy nation, a people belonging to God, that you may declare the praises of him who called you out of darkness into his wonderful light" (I Peter 2:9).

As we learn to use our time, talents, and treasure for his glory and for his purposes, we are genuinely delighted when we see lives changed by our efforts. In perhaps the most memorable moment of the film, *Chariots of Fire,* Eric Liddell and his sister Jenny stand on a hill near Edinburgh, Scotland. Jenny can't understand why Eric is so dedicated to running in the Olympics when so many "more important things" need his attention. After she states her case, Eric looks at her and explains, "Jenny, Jenny. God made me fast, and when I run, I feel his pleasure."

When we are gripped with our calling, when we are devoted to God's purposes, and when we are actively using our abilities to serve him, we "feel his pleasure." We enjoy the Lord, and we enjoy the role he has entrusted to us in expanding his kingdom.

Before we begin to pursue the bold strategies that can transform a life, a church, and a community for Christ, we need to be gripped with a strong, clear calling. We dare not place anything else before this calling—not even the needs of people around us, and definitely not the desire to play an important role and win the applause of others. God's call is a summons to respond to his greatness and grace, to first devote ourselves completely to him and then to his purposes. In the next chapter, we will examine how a heart of faith responds to God's clear call.

At the end of each chapter, you will find some questions and exercises to help you apply the principles in the chapter. Don't hurry through these. Your times of reflection may be the most valuable benefits of reading this book. Take time to answer the questions by yourself. Then, if other leaders in your church are also reading this book, use the reflection sections as the basis of rich discussions so you can chart a new course for your church.

We have provided only small spaces in these reflection sections. You may need a separate journal to write your thoughts that are prodded by these questions and exercises.

Reflection

1. Use your own words to paraphrase Os Guinness' definition of calling: "Calling is the truth that God calls us to himself so decisively that everything we are, everything we do, and everything we have is invested with a special devotion and dynamism lived out as a response to his summons and service."

2. Proverb 28:1 says, "The wicked man flees though no one pursues, but the righteous are as bold as a lion." What are some reasons safety is so attractive?

How do you distinguish between God-inspired boldness and prideful ambition?

3. Reread the portion of "Law of the Yukon" quoted in this chapter. What are some similarities between the Yukon miners and our roles as Christian leaders?

Does this poem inspire you? Why or why not?

4. Have you ever sensed that God might be prompting you to dream bigger dreams for him? Explain your answer.

chapter 2

Focus: One Thing I Do

"But one thing I do: Forgetting what is behind and straining toward what is ahead, I press on toward the goal to win the prize for which God has called me heavenward in Christ Jesus" (Phil 3:13-14).

I am often fascinated to see what motivates people—what brings fire to their eyes and color to their cheeks. I love to see someone get excited about an idea, a vision, or a dream.

However, sometimes people are naïve in their expectations. They believe they can just wish something, and somehow God will make it happen. Paul was under no such illusions. His clear vision was coupled with a strong grasp of the reality of hardships, opposition, and heartache that would accompany his pursuit of God's plan for him. But none of those things diverted him from his single-minded focus. Like all of us, he had plenty of responsibilities, but only one thing consumed his heart. He wrote to the Philippian believers, "But one thing I do: Forgetting what is behind and straining toward what is ahead, I press on toward the goal to win the prize for which God has called me heavenward in Christ Jesus" (Phil 3:13-14).

What gave Paul such a clear focus on his life's purpose? Earlier in the same letter, he had listed all his accomplishments and titles. He had been the number one man in Judaism, the ultimate corporate climber, the hero of his time, but none of that mattered after he met Christ. He explained, "But whatever was to my profit I now consider loss for the sake of Christ. What is more, I consider everything a loss compared to the surpassing greatness of knowing Christ Jesus my Lord" (Phil 3:7-8).

Paul's response to God's calling was first and foremost to love and follow Christ himself. This should be the response of every believer— not just pastors, missionaries, and church workers. The depth and breadth of our response is shaped by the extent of our awe for the One who is calling us. Os Guinness writes, "God calls people to himself, but this call is no casual suggestion. He is so awe inspiring and his summons so commanding that only one response is appropriate—a response as total and universal as the authority of the Caller."[5]

Our delight in the love of God and our passion to please him come from our reverence for the awe-inspiring greatness and grace of God. Christ's call to us, however, does not always arrive during silent moments. We have to listen

Our delight in the love of God and our passion to please him come from our reverence for the awe-inspiring greatness and grace of God.

intently because it may come amid the din of hundreds of other invitations around us, including opportunities to get what we want by having more possessions or money, to climb the ladder of success, or to gain power over others. A few of these messages are clearly seductive and evil, but numerous others are good things that create problems only when they take first place in our lives: the affection of a spouse, the joy of children, the enjoyment of seeing success in business or any other field. If we appreciate these as gifts from

---

5   Guinness, *The Call*, p. 30.

God, they retain their proper place, but if they become central in our hearts, they take the place of God and become idols.

This is not a new problem. Through Jeremiah, God lamented the misplaced allegiance of his people,

"My people have committed two sins:
They have forsaken me,
    the spring of living water,
and have dug their own cisterns,
    broken cisterns that cannot hold water"
(Jer 2:13).

Without a clear, unmistakable call from God, first to a focused relationship with him and then to determining exactly what he wants us to do, we vainly search for meaning or we give up and drift in meaninglessness. Some of us "dig our own cisterns" by continually trying to prove ourselves. We are intent on being successful, but not for Christ's sake. We are threatened by failure, so we avoid it at any cost. We may work 80 hours a week, compulsively focus on details, or blame others whenever something goes wrong.

Others give up on having any real meaning in life. Even some people in positions of Christian leadership feel deep emptiness and simply go through the motions of ministry. They are bored, without drive, without dreams, and without hope. And others are still hoping to find meaning by trying a little of this and a little of that to see if anything stimulates them. Genuine calling is a powerful antidote to the drive to prove ourselves,

> *Genuine calling is a powerful antidote to the drive to prove ourselves, the emptiness of boredom or discouragement, and the meaninglessness of superficial, scattered activities.*

the emptiness of boredom or discouragement, and the meaninglessness of superficial, scattered activities.

Calling is not about the size of a church, the scope of a ministry, or the bottom line for a Christian business person—it is about the heart of God. Many people miss this crucial point. We can get so hung up on building a large ministry or business that we focus on comparing ourselves with others instead of loving and serving Jesus Christ. It is a personal and an organizational tragedy to forget that the root, the source, and the heart of our calling is that we have been chosen, forgiven, and adopted by God. We miss it all if we bypass the warm, rich, powerful relationship that must be the center of who we are and what we do. Without it, all our efforts are only to build our own kingdoms, not God's—to please ourselves, not him.

> *His love and purpose are so encouraging, comforting, and compelling that our greatest delight is knowing and serving him.*

The Shorter Version of the Westminster Catechism states, "The chief end of man is to glorify God and enjoy Him forever." Our highest calling, in fact, the very reason we were created, is to bring honor to the sovereign and loving God of the universe. But that's not all. His love and purpose are so encouraging, comforting, and compelling that our greatest delight is knowing and serving him. Activity that flows out of our identity as beloved children of God is good, right, and wonderful, but activity that attempts to prove ourselves eats away at our hearts and ultimately leaves us empty and deeply disappointed. We won't have completely pure motives until we see Christ face to face, so we need to continually cast ourselves at his feet, to soak up his grace, and ask him to purify our hearts and give us a genuine and deep desire to please him.

I recommend two books that point people powerfully to the heart of God: J. I. Packer's *Knowing God* and Henry Blackaby's *Experiencing God*. As we draw close to God and experience his goodness and greatness, we have the incredible privilege of being his ambassadors and his soldiers. That's the beginning point of our calling, and it is the continuous fountain of motivation for the rest of our lives.

Peter makes this point simply and powerfully:

"His divine power has given us everything we need for life and godliness through our knowledge of him who called us by his own glory and goodness. Through these he has given us his very great and precious promises, so that through them you may participate in the divine nature and escape the corruption in the world caused by evil desires" (II Peter 1:3-4).

Let me give you some examples of people who have responded to God's call, his "very great and precious promises," and now participate in his divine nature and his divine work.

Bob Buford accumulated great wealth through his cable television business, but he dedicated all he had and all he is to fulfill God's calling in his life. He founded an organization called Leadership Network, which has shaped the lives and ministries of thousands of Christian leaders over the past decade. Bob's book *Halftime* details the journey we all can make by moving from a focus on "success" to a focus on "significance."

In the middle of the 19th century, a poor cobbler wanted his life to count for God. He asked his pastor if he could teach Sunday school, but his pastor said, "No." This cobbler persisted in requesting a place to serve, and finally the pastor told him he could teach a class of rowdy, recalcitrant boys—the ones nobody else wanted. The man gladly taught these boys the message of the gospel and imparted the love of God to them. One of those who trusted Christ under the cobbler's care was Dwight L. Moody, who became the most famous gospel preacher of his day.

My brother Gene is a successful businessman who could have had great wealth, but he chose to use everything he has to build God's kingdom instead of his own. I could tell many details of his generosity, but he would be embarrassed. Let me say only that God has used him in a powerful way to begin our church in Carson Valley, to fund many other ministries, and to provide godly leadership as he uses his abilities and gifts to honor the Lord.

Joni Eareckson Tada would have been just another nice, pretty Christian girl, but a tragic accident as a teenager left her a quadriplegic. She could have lapsed into depression and self-pity for the rest of her life, but she trusted that God could still use her to accomplish his will. She put her broken body into his hands. Today, she is a living inspiration to any of us who feel we've gotten a raw deal from life or from God. She is the founder and president of Joni and Friends, a ministry designed to meet the needs of disabled people. Her perspective is, "I am dedicated to the Master. He can use my strengths and my disabilities for his glory." She can't walk and she has someone brush her teeth and change her clothes for her, but she still trusts God to use her to accomplish his sovereign will to advance his kingdom.

Laura Saintey is a member of our church who has a bachelor's degree in special education and 15 years' teaching experience. Laura could use her time in any way she wants, but she chooses over and over again to use her many skills to serve the Lord. The last time I saw her she was constructing our Easter drama stage with a belt sander in her hand and a big grin on her face. Serving God is not drudgery to her. She is thrilled that God is willing to use every talent he has given her—even belt sanding!

I recall the story of an American who visited a missionary in Korea. As the two men walked together in the country, they observed a man and his son in a rice field. The son was struggling to pull the small plow in front of his father. The American visitor commented, "What incredible poverty! I can't believe that boy is having to pull a plow." The missionary shook his head and explained, "You don't understand. The man and his family are members of our church. When we needed money to build a new building, the man gave his ox to us. What you see is not poverty, but heart-felt dedication to Christ."

At the End of the Day

The Scriptures tell us two events will finalize the eternal destiny of every person who has ever lived. Two key passages describe a tragic day when unbelievers will be judged: Matthew 25 and Revelation 20. But believers will also have their "day in court." In both of Paul's letters to the Corinthians he explains how they will come before the Judgment Seat of Christ. On that day, each of our thoughts, words, and deeds since trusting Christ as our Savior will be evaluated. Those things we have done for selfish reasons will burn up, like "wood, hay or straw," but those things we have done for Christ will be remembered and rewarded.

In Matthew 25, Jesus told a parable about a man who entrusted his property to three servants prior to going on a journey. One servant received five talents, another two, and another one. When the man returned, he called the servants and asked them to give an account of their stewardship. The one who had been given five talents had made five more, and the one who had two had made two more. They heard the treasured words from their master, "Well done." The servant who had only one talent, though, had been afraid of his master and had buried his talent in the ground. The master rebuked this servant, not for taking a risk and losing his money, but for not taking a risk at all. The master scolded him, "At least you could have put in it in the bank and earned some interest!" Risk is a part of life. The only servant who was declared "wicked" and "lazy" was the one who cowered in fear and refused to take a risk.

The servants in this parable symbolize you and me. God has given some of us incredible abilities, and he has given others of us more modest talents. But each of us is provided with *some* amount of God-given talent to use for his kingdom. God doesn't compare us to each other; he simply asks us to give an account of how we've used what he has given us. Jesus' parable converges with Paul's teaching about the Judgement Seat of Christ. A day will come when you and I, like the two faithful servants who took risks for their master's sake, will stand before our Master to give an account of our faithfulness to Christ and his cause. On that day, I long to hear the words, "Well done, good and faithful servant. Enter into the joy of your Master."

> *"Well done, good and faithful servant. Enter into the joy of your Master."*

Leadership Demands Taking Risks

Some of us are bold as lions; some as timid as mice. Genuine leadership, however, demands that we take reasonable risks that offer the hope of great gain for those we lead. Helen Keller had every earthly reason to be a mouse, but she had the heart of a lion. She spoke boldly, "Security is mostly a superstition. It does not exist in nature, nor do the children of men as a whole experience it. Avoiding danger is no safer in the long run than outright exposure. Life is either a daring adventure or nothing."

Christian leaders come in all shapes and types. Many studies have been conducted to identify leadership styles. For our purposes, we will distinguish four types: commander, coach, counselor, and calculator. Let's examine how each type handles risks.

— The *commander* enjoys taking risks because he (or she) sees them as necessary for progress. This person envisions big goals and marshals the troops to accomplish them. He is practical and logical in outlining the steps to get where he wants to go. In volunteer organizations such as churches, commanders need to understand that not everybody is goal-oriented. Many people feel threatened by risk, so a wise commander takes time to inform, motivate, and encourage those with whom he works.

— The *coach* loves to see others succeed. While he (or she) may be perfectly capable of getting a job done himself, the risk involved is in letting someone else step up and do it. Rather than relying on personal magnetism and enthusiasm, the coach motivates people to face risks by taking time to clearly explain the goals, roles, and strategies of the project at hand. A coach is enthusiastic about challenges, but he may not always think through all the details of accomplishing his goal.

— The *counselor* is fulfilled by developing an overall strategy that may be very complex, and then helping others understand their roles in accomplishing the plan. A degree of risk may be necessary at times, but counselors are more comfortable when they play an important part to think, research, and develop the strategy. This type of leader is usually very patient and persistent, but is annoyed or threatened when his coworkers demonstrate excessive optimism or unreasonable uses of power.

— The *calculator* is a numbers-cruncher who finds satisfaction in following clearly outlined systems and procedures. This person is very conscientious and insists that things be done the "right way." The calculator avoids risks whenever possible by minimizing change and sticking to rigid rules.

Every person can be a leader, but some are more gifted than others in defining groundbreaking purposes and motivating others to accomplish stated goals. Dr. Dan Reiland, the Executive Pastor at Crossroads Community Church in Lawrenceville, Georgia, observed, "Great leaders possess a mix of an entrepreneurial spirit, the mind of a dreamer, and a compelling strategic vision that sets the overall tone and direction of an organization. They see a clear and preferred picture of the future without prompting from others. They have a passion to see the vision come true even in the face of opposition. . . . One thing I have observed about the vast majority of visionaries is that they deeply value people and a better way of living for those people. However, this value is not necessarily on an individual level; it is more on a big picture/organizational level or 'for the masses' level. Lest this sound dispassionate, they are often willing to take great risks and make great sacrifices to see the vision become reality."[6]

Reiland explains that very few people possess the gifts to be *natural* visionaries who dream dreams that have never been conceived before. The rest of us, however, can acknowledge such people and learn from them. Our own dreams can be enriched, broadened, deepened, and strengthened by rubbing shoulders with (or reading articles and books by) these remarkably gifted few. The rest of us, then, are *learned* visionaries.

---

6   Dr. Dan Reiland, "The Pastor's Coach," INJOY Insights, Volume 3, Issue 13, July 2002.

Wisdom and Risks

Christian leaders may gravitate toward business as usual and avoid risks for several reasons: their criteria for "success" may be set far too low; they haven't seen a go-for-it leader in action; they are bogged down in personal problems; they haven't been in a leadership position long enough to feel comfortable; or they want to win loyalty before they try anything new. But avoiding risks at all costs is not true leadership. Wisdom is necessary to determine which risks are worthwhile and which are foolish.

Risk itself is not a goal of leadership. It is simply a reality for those who have a large vision. In II Timothy 2, Paul uses three metaphors to describe church leaders: soldier, athlete, and farmer. People in each of these three roles work toward a specific purpose: to please the commanding officer and win the battle, to win the race, or to enjoy the proceeds of the harvest. But all three roles also have inherent risks. The soldier endures hardship and risks injury or death, the athlete risks public failure, and the farmer risks floods, drought, insect and bird damage, and other perpetual problems. (Many leaders can relate to the courage and perseverance of the farmer, whose last crop may have been eaten by locusts, but who takes the risk to borrow money and start yet another crop.)

> *Risk itself is not a goal of leadership. It is simply a reality for those who have a large vision.*

Adventure Requires Tenacity

We may endure hardship and take risks for many reasons, some good and some bad, but the development of godly character is all that counts on that day when we stand before Christ. Insecure people are often driven to succeed in order to please others. Tenacity without character may allow some success in the short term, but it always sows the seeds of eventual destruction. Secure, mature people do the right things for the right reasons and endure hardship simply because they are following the right path, not because that path is easy.

Whenever, I speak to parents, I tell them, "Please don't tell your children that it is easier to do right. That may not be true. Doing right may require incredible courage and a willingness to face ridicule and rejection." Following God's call is certainly an adventure, but adventures, by their nature, involve difficulty and danger.

If we are convinced of the rightness of our cause, we will be willing to endure, not because of gain or fame, but because God has a claim on our lives. Knowing which risks to pursue always goes back to the heart of God, his calling for us to honor him, and the sobering fact that someday we will stand before the Master to give an account of how we responded to his call.

Teddy Roosevelt was a man of adventure in ranching, hunting, and politics. He said, "No man is worth his salt who is not ready at all times to risk his body, to risk his well-being, to risk his life, in a great cause." The same spirit of adventure is required for spiritual leaders as well. In his classic work, *Spiritual Leadership,* Oswald Sanders wrote, "The real qualities of leadership are to be found in those who are willing to suffer for the sake of objectives great enough to demand their wholehearted obedience."[7]

Jack London's books are epic stories of men and women on their way to the Yukon goldfields. If they chose the water route along the coast of Alaska and then upriver, they had to brave the storms in the Bering Sea and ice in the Yukon River that threatened to tear holes in their boats. If they

---

7   J. Oswald Sanders, *Spiritual Leadership,* (Moody Press, Chicago, IL, 1967), p. 17.

took the overland trail, they faced long miles of trudging through mud and snow, through swollen, snow-melt-filled rivers and over almost impenetrable mountains. Many died just attempting to get to the boomtowns. Once they were there, they had to brave long days of backbreaking labor and long nights in lean-to cabins with their companions. Injury in those isolated places often meant death. Still, they came by the thousands. The journey was dangerous and the work was difficult, but those men and women believed they would find gold. The hope of finding that gold was worth any sacrifice or hardship.

Is our hope any less than theirs? Theirs was temporal; ours is eternal. However, they had one distinct advantage: they could see and touch their treasure. Ours, though, is unseen. We need God to open the eyes of our hearts so we can see with great clarity the reality of our spiritual treasure. Then we, like the Yukon miners, will gladly endure every hardship and any sacrifice to obtain the treasure God has for us. This kind of hope is what drives us to press on toward the goal to win the prize for which God has called us.

Reflection

1. What previous experiences have put light in your eyes and fire in your soul? Describe a couple of times you've experienced this kind of passion in ministry.

2. Reflect on this passage:

   "But one thing I do: Forgetting what is behind and straining toward what is ahead, I press on toward the goal to win the prize for which God has called me heavenward in Christ Jesus" (Phil 3:13-14).

   What does this passage say to you about God's calling and your need to focus your attention?

3. Review the four types of leaders in this chapter (commander, coach, counselor, calculator). Which are you? How do people in your group usually handle risks?

4. What insights and experiences have helped you develop tenacity? How does tenacity relate to vision?

chapter 3

Forming the Vision

"When the servant of the man of God got up and went out early the next morning, an army with horses and chariots had surrounded the city. 'Oh, my lord, what shall we do?' the servant asked.

'Don't be afraid,' the prophet answered. 'Those who are with us are more than those who are with them'" (II Kings 6:15-16).

In his popular book, *Wild at Heart,* John Eldridge says that God created us for adventure. In fact, we only find true fulfillment when we are willing to take risks to see great things happen. "Small dreams," one man said, "do not enflame the hearts of men." A vision begins with the conviction that what currently exists isn't enough. We long for more. We want to see change. We yearn for something far better. The process of forming a clear vision begins with hearing from God. We need to be touched by his love, discover his perspective on the needs around us, and acknowledge his willingness to accomplish his purposes through us.

We can learn a valuable lesson from the story of Elisha found in II Kings 6:8-23. The nation was at war, and the enemy had sent "a strong force" with the sole purpose of capturing Elisha. When Elisha's servant walked outside that morning in Dothan, all he saw were the hordes of enemy chariots and horses. He was terrified and desperate! But Elisha had God's perspective and told his servant, "Don't be afraid. Those who are with us [the unseen hosts of God] are more than those who are with them."

Good spiritual leaders have the ability to "see the unseen," to use God-given insight that looks beyond the tangible, physical world and recognizes the presence, purposes, and power of God, even in the most distressing and seemingly hopeless situations. Oswald Sanders observed, "Those who have most powerfully and permanently influenced their generation have been 'seers'—men who have seen more and farther than others. (They are) men of faith, for faith is vision. This was true of the prophets or seers of the Old Testament times. Moses, one of the greatest leaders of all time, 'endured as seeing him who is invisible.' His faith imparted vision. Elisha's servant saw with great vividness the vastness of the encircling army. Elisha saw the invincible environing host of heaven who were invisible to his servant. His faith imparted vision."[8]

Three Crucial Elements of the Vision

God's call in our lives is shaped by three crucial elements which together form our vision of how he will use us. They are: our *grasp* of the heart of God (which determines our motivation), our *grip* on the needs of people around us (which shapes the direction of our service), and the *gifts* God has given us (which determine the effectiveness of our service).

These three factors are not linear. We don't first fully grasp the heart of God, then examine where to serve, and finally use our talents. Rather, these elements are interwoven and enhance each other. As we see God use us, our understanding of his grace deepens and we become even more committed to meeting the needs of those around us. This diagram shows the vital connections of these three elements of calling.

---

8   Sanders, *Spiritual Leadership*, p. 48.

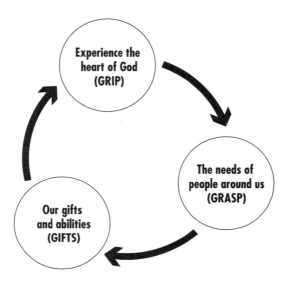

We should never take our motivations for granted. We never get beyond the temptation to become proud, selfish, or lazy. No matter how long we've been believers or how successful we've been, we should never stop asking ourselves, "Am I being faithful to the Father? Am I answering his call or am I pleasing myself?" This reflection is not destructive, guilt-ridden, morbid introspection; it is a right and reasonable analysis. It is the same honesty that David exhibited when he prayed,

"Search me, O God, and know my heart;
　　test me and know my anxious thoughts.
See if there is any offensive way in me,
　　and lead me in the way everlasting" (Ps 139:23-24).

The previous two chapters focused on the heart of God and his compelling call for each of us to respond in wholehearted, glad obedience because of his unsearchable greatness and grace. His claim on our lives is total and reasonable. As our hearts are gripped more completely through the process of spiritual growth, we long to please him more and more. Our early attempts to serve him are checkered with successes and failures, just as a child learns to walk or anyone learns a new skill.

In time, we find that some aspects of our service are met with unusual successes. People come to Christ, we excel in organizing activities, or those we lead feel encouraged and find meaning in their service. These and countless other successes show us that God has empowered us with spiritual gifts to serve him in specific roles in the body of Christ. (See Romans 12, I Corinthians 12, Ephesians 4, and I Peter 4.)

Now we want to look at the third element in how our vision is formed: the needs of people in our communities.

The Desperate Need for Change

As our hearts grow increasingly in tune with God's heart, our eyes will be opened to needs around us. We may have previously ignored the hurting people around us because we were too busy accomplishing our own goals or too overwhelmed with our own problems. But as we experience God's love and strength, we become more secure, our motives are purified, and we are able to see others through eyes of compassion.

We want to change lives. But few of us do the homework necessary to identify the open doors to the gospel currently available in our culture.

A clear assessment of needs is crucial as God forms his vision for our lives. One church leader lamented that most of us make assumptions rather than looking closely at our communities. And when we generalize, we miss the specifics. Bill Hybels of Willow Creek Community Church has commented sadly, "It is a blight on the church that the average McDonalds' owner knows more about his community than we do." All a franchise owner wants to do is sell burgers and fries. We want to change lives. But few of us do the homework necessary to identify the open doors to the gospel currently available in our culture.

Also, many of us have spiritualized our ministries so much that we have become poor students of our mission field. We piously say that God will work through us, but we don't take the time to research demographic patterns, to ask questions, to study trends, or to read the reports from the Chamber of Commerce. Trusting God, however, doesn't imply pious passivity. Paul was anything but passive. He was a serious student of those to whom he ministered. Jesus also tailored his messages to his audiences. To the Pharisees, he spoke of self-righteousness and grace. To the common people, he spoke in parables about farming and the seasons. To the lost, he told stories of being found. We, too, need to become excellent students of those we hope to reach. Entrepreneurs make their living by responding to the needs of their community. They can often help their pastors perceive their community more accurately.

We live in an age of tolerance that is eroding the foundations of our faith. Fifty years ago, parents taught their children to be tolerant of those who were different. Tolerating differences was a way to show love to them. But today, that term has taken a very different twist. It is now used throughout our educational system to mean that every belief, no matter how bizarre, has equally value. Young people are taught to "tolerate" other faiths and practices, which sounds good and reasonable on the surface. But one result is that the cutting edge of truth is seen as a threat, and those who teach standards of right and wrong are considered to be intolerant, the worst criticism imaginable in this age of intellectual and spiritual mush.

Another result of this watering down of truth is that many people consider themselves to be Christians without knowing what that means. One study by George Barna found that 67 percent of unchurched adults, approximately 65 to 70 million people in the United States, call themselves Christians. More than a third claim to have a personal commitment to Christ, and 40 percent of the unchurched report that their faith is important to them. However, their beliefs are quite shaky. Barna reports:

- 64% of the unchurched say that Satan is not a living being but only a symbol of evil.
- 64% of unchurched adults state that a good person can earn his or her way into heaven.
- 44% of the unchurched define God as an entity other than the perfect, all-powerful, all-knowing Creator of the universe who continues to rule his creation today.
- 48% of the unchurched assert that when Jesus Christ lived on earth, he committed sins.
- Only 22% of the unchurched firmly believe that the Bible is totally accurate in all that it teaches.[9]

The conclusion is inescapable. Great numbers who claim to be Christians are actually a significant mission field for the church. Because they are inoculated by a watered-down version of Christianity, it can be more difficult to reach them with genuine truth. The good news is that many people in our neighborhoods, shops, offices, farms, and factories have a generally positive view of Jesus Christ. They desperately need us to take the initiative to tell them about—and demonstrate—the transforming grace and power of Christ.

Sadly, the erosion of truth and commitment is not limited those who seldom darken the doors of our churches. Another Barna study conducted among church-going

---

9   www.barna.org/cgibin/PageCategory.asp?CategoryID=38

believers reveals that their biblical understanding and will-ingness to live out their faith is remarkably shallow. These shocking statistics are found in Barna's book on the state of discipleship in America (*Growing True Disciples,* Waterbrook Press, 2001).

- When Christian adults were asked to identify the most important goal for their life, not a single person said it was to be a committed follower of Jesus Christ, or to make disciples of Christ.
- Fewer than one out of every five born again adults had any specific and measurable goals related to their personal spiritual development.
- Less than one percent of all believers perceived a connection between their efforts to worship God and their development as a disciple of Jesus.
- The most widely known Bible verse among adult and teen believers is "God helps those who help themselves"—which is not in the Bible, and actually conflicts with the basic message of Scripture.
- Only a minority of adult and teen believers contend that absolute moral truth exists.
- Fewer than one out of every ten believers possesses a biblical worldview as the basis for his or her decision-making or behavior.
- When given 13 basic teachings from the Bible, only one percent of adult believers firmly embraced all 13 as being biblical perspectives.
- Research revealed specific and significant problems related to core spiritual practices such as worship, evangelism, stewardship, community service, and lifestyles.

Barna commented that most people don't feel their church helps them grow spiritually in any meaningful way. He wrote, "Few believers said that their church lacked programs, but most Christians complained that little is done to effectively motivate and facilitate their development as genuine, fervent followers of Christ. Our surveys among pastors showed that they dismissed such views as excuses and as inaccurate, but the bottom line remains unchanged: most Christians are simply not making progress in their personal spiritual development."[10]

Responding to These Facts

How are we to feel when we read such troubling reports? Do we shake our heads and simply go about our business as usual, or are our hearts broken by the emptiness of lives and the deception of the enemy? When Jesus was on his way into Jerusalem during his last week on earth, he looked around the city. The needs of the people—the ones who would first praise him and later yell, "Crucify him!"—broke his heart. He cried out, "O Jerusalem, Jerusalem, you who kill the prophets and stone those sent to you, how often I have longed to gather your children together, as a hen gathers her chicks under her wings, but you were not willing" (Matt 23:37). Do you hear the pain in his words? The people he longed to touch with his grace included not only those who were sweet, but also the self-righteous, the cruel, the bitter, and the vicious. Jesus wept for them all.

Do we shake our heads and simply go about our business as usual, or are our hearts broken by the emptiness of lives and the deception of the enemy?

Some of us haven't wept enough lately. We see so much crime and violence on television that we are numbed by it and

---

10 www.barna.org/cgibin/PagePressRelease.asp?PressReleaseID=76& Reference=E&Key=discipleship

isolate ourselves. Our hearts haven't been broken by the needs of others. Oh, we may be near those who are hurting and even offer comfort to them, but we have insulated our hearts from really grasping the depth of their despair.

I'm convinced that none of us, even the most compassionate among us, can maintain that level of empathy in relationships with needy people all day every day. Jesus slipped away from the crowds to take retreats in the hills or by the seashore with his trusted disciples. Those were times to reflect on their experiences, to recharge their sense of purpose, and replenish their hearts for the Father and for other people. If you and I are going to remain spiritually alert and genuinely compassionate, we also need times to recharge our spiritual engines. The price of spiritual numbness is too high . . . for us and for those we love and serve.

We often look for God's direction during our mountaintop experiences, but sometimes he uses the pits of despair to provide us with clearer vision. In my own experience, that day in the snow while on a retreat was anything but a mountaintop experience. I was desperate for God to show me his will and give me direction. Then, even when he spoke clearly to my heart, I said "No" to him, adding guilt to my desperation. But not for long. Eventually my desperation was turned into clear direction and guilt was transformed into thankfulness and freedom. It all started, though, in the valley.

Isaiah was entrusted with a message of despair to deliver to the children of God. The prophecies in the first 39 chapters of his book told of physical destruction and devastation, and this message crushed his own spirit. When God showed him how Jerusalem would be destroyed and the people captured, Isaiah's heart was broken. He wanted to run away and hide. He wrote:

"Therefore I said, 'Turn away from me;
    let me weep bitterly.
Do not try to console me
    over the destruction of my people.'
The Lord, the Lord Almighty, has a day
    of tumult and trampling and terror
    in the Valley of Vision,
A day of battering down walls
    and of crying out to the mountains" (Is 22:4-5).

God's purpose for us is often clarified in the "Valley of Vision," a place where our hearts are broken by the devastation we see in lives around us. But make no mistake; our task is not to dispassionately acknowledge the hurts in people's lives like we are taking a census. Our task is to see the needs of people through the eyes of Christ, to understand that his heart breaks as he looks at divorce, bitterness, disease, death, and empty lives. The more we are in tune with God's heart, the more our hearts will break, too, when we see the needs of others around us. The wonderful news for Isaiah and for us is that the story doesn't end with chapter 39. The rest of Isaiah's writing tells of the invasion of the Spirit of God and the Servant of God to rescue people from sin and give them hope and healing. We hold both in our hands: the desperate needs of people as well as the incredible purpose and power of God to change lives. Both are necessary parts of a clear, godly, passionate vision that changes lives—ours and others'.

We hold both in our hands: the desperate needs of people as well as the incredible purpose and power of God to change lives.

The church can continue to go along doing business as usual for about another decade, but by then, the alarming trend toward irrelevance will have taken a tragic toll. By then we will have become so marginalized that we will cease to have a significant impact on our culture and on individuals. Those who have traveled to Great Britain in recent years and have observed the spiritual barrenness of that country wonder what happened to the Christ-centered zeal that gripped England when God used people like Wesley and Spurgeon to enflame hearts for Christ. Today, America is where Britain was in about 1870 when it still had some dynamic ministries, but the church was losing its voice by becoming irrelevant. If we don't change course soon in America, we will slide down the same slippery slope and become a part of history instead of being a powerful force for God and for good.

The United States loses an average of 72 churches each week as 24 open their doors for the first time—a net loss of 48 churches per week. If we slide toward irrelevance, most of our churches will stay open, but they will be populated by those who value tradition, not zeal for the cause of Christ. Facing the facts and making necessary changes to stay relevant in a changing culture requires that church leaders take risks, if not for ourselves, for the sake of our children and grandchildren. Their spiritual lives will be influenced by our actions today. We need pastors and entrepreneurs who will answer the call!

The problem is that many church leaders are already overwhelmed with just maintaining the status quo. They are busy with the problems in their communities, their churches, their families, and their own lives. The idea that they need to make radical changes that will have an impact on future generations is not even on the first three pages of their "To Do" lists. But it needs to be. We need a fresh infusion of faith to believe that Christ really changes lives. Then God will use the community of believers to reparent those whose lives are shattered by abuse, abandonment, and addiction, and he will use that fellowship of the faithful to impart meaning to those who have lost hope.

Positive changes will never take place as long as we bury our heads and keep doing business as usual. They happen only when we open our eyes to see the desperate needs around us and then trust our merciful God to use us to touch broken hearts and mend shattered relationships. A dynamic group of Christians doesn't just tell people what to do. It also shows people how the Christian life is lived, by rigorous examples of love, service, and sacrifice. Jesus didn't just tell his disciples what to do. He showed them over and over again. The bad news is that they were so slow to catch on. The good news is that they eventually got it (with one exception), and this motley crew literally changed the world.

Not long ago, our church made some key chains to give to people who attend our services. The inscription reads simply, "Changed lives are our business." A church that makes assumptions about the needs of people misses its target as often as it hits it. That may have been good enough years ago when the church held a more prominent role in our culture, but it's not good enough today. We need to be students of our culture broadly and our communities specifically so our prayers and our programs are designed to touch the real needs of those who have been entrusted to our care by Almighty God. Insight into people's needs gives us direction, being in touch with the heart of God gives us passion, using the abilities he has given us makes us effective, and ministering in community provides the dynamic of rich relationships that changes lives.

"Changed lives are our business."

A Few Examples

The Scriptures, church history, and our own experiences reveal some wonderful examples of people who have responded to God's call to serve him by meeting the needs of others. Jesus used every circumstance and every relationship to show his disciples how God wanted to use them to meet needs. They often misunderstood (I find that encouraging!), but he never stopped demonstrating the heart of God in action.

One day the disciples came back from McDonalds (or the first-century equivalent) with lunch to find Jesus talking to a Samaritan adulteress, and they wondered what in the world he was doing. As always, he took that opportunity to teach them about the Father's grace and the needs of people. When they asked if he was hungry, he told them, "I have food to eat that you know nothing about." They probably wondered if he had a candy bar in his pocket, but he explained, "My food is to do the will of him who sent me and to finish his work." He continued, "Do you not say, 'Four months more and then the harvest?' I tell you, open your eyes and look at the fields! They are ripe for harvest" (John 4:35). Of course, the harvest he was talking about was all of humanity, including the Samaritan woman and her friends and family. The disciples had been concerned with the things of this life, but Jesus demonstrated and taught that the needs of people, even despised Samaritans, is the business of heaven. The Twelve just needed eyes to see all that God could do.

When Saul was king of Israel, the Philistines attacked the land. At that time, Saul's army was tiny and weak, but his son Jonathan was as brave as a lion. The desperate needs of the nation called him to action. The young man took his armorbearer and walked out toward the mighty enemy army. He told his attendant, "Come, let's go over to the outpost of those uncircumcised fellows. Perhaps the Lord will act in our behalf. Nothing can hinder the Lord from saving, whether by many or by few" (I Sam 14:6). I love that attitude! Jonathan didn't know what would happen. He told his armorbearer, "Perhaps the Lord will act." If God worked a miracle, the army and the nation might be saved. If not. . . . The situation was desperate, so Jonathan acted at the risk of his own life. God honored his faith and courage with an incredible victory.

John Knox was a Scottish pastor who saw the spiritual blindness of the people. His heart broke for them. The intensity of his love for God and his desire for God to use him to touch lives in his native land is forever immortalized in his passionate prayer, "Give me Scotland or I die!"

The commitment of hundreds of thousands, if not millions, of people has been galvanized by the life of Jim Elliott. His young wife Elisabeth wrote of Jim's joy of serving and his determination to honor Christ above all else in her book, *Shadow of the Almighty*. His zeal for Christ led him and three other young men to attempt to make connections with the Auca Indians in Ecuador. His death at their hands was considered a "waste" by many at the time, but in the years since that day when four brave young missionaries died, countless men and women have been moved by their example. Thousands have responded to the needs of lost people and the call of Christ to take the gospel to the ends of the world.

Not everyone who is gripped by the love of God and the needs of people becomes as well known as Jim Elliott, but numerous others serve God with that wonderful blend of tears and laughter. They are deeply moved by the hurts in people's lives, and their ever-deepening experience of the heart of God compels them to love, give, and serve with endurance and joy. God is using them according to the talents, gifts, abilities, and resources he has entrusted to them.

Two Specific Areas of Needs

At Carson Valley Christian Center over the past few years, God has been leading us to focus on two areas of ministry to touch the needs of people in our community: sports and recovery ministries. Like many areas of the country, ours is crazy about sports. People may not care much about coming to hear a message from the Bible, but they are very interested in a program that lets them or their children participate in sports.

For example, a man in our church, Kevin Schaller, is a third-degree black belt in karate. He has wanted to use his skills to have an impact on people for Christ, so a couple of years ago, he asked if our church would sponsor a karate class. We expected a dozen or so people to attend, but to our pleasant surprise, we've had more than 200 people participate. Kevin has used his skills not just to impart abilities in martial arts, but to impart the gospel of Christ. He has been thrilled with the response, and our church has grown because of his creativity and commitment.

Decades ago it might have been possible to meet several people without encountering anyone who had been devastated by divorce, alcohol, drugs, or abuse. Today, however, those problems are widespread and affect a majority of our population. Of course, the addicts and perpetrators desperately need a safe and powerful environment to experience grace and truth so they can rebuild their lives. But victims and family members also need help.

Churches simply must speak to these needs or risk irrelevance. Some leaders are hesitant to enter into the world of felt needs because they are afraid of getting off track. Perhaps they've heard stories of New Age techniques being used or of support groups becoming "pity parties." But the needs are real. Leaders need to do the necessary research to find curriculum that is sound and biblical, and to train leaders who genuinely love God and lead people to him for forgiveness, truth, and healing. We've found that these groups are some of the most powerful places for the message of the gospel to be imparted to needy people. In fact, some churches report that more people come to Christ through these ministries than every other avenue in the church combined!

We can keep doing business as usual in our churches so that we avoid risk and feel comfortable with incremental change, or we can ask God to open our eyes to the powerful confluence of his heart, the needs of people, and the spiritual gifts he has entrusted to us so that we are passionate, directed, and effective for him and his kingdom.

Apple Computer founder Steve Jobs once asked, "Do you want to spend the rest of your life selling sugared water, or do you want to change the world?" He was talking about computers changing the world, and indeed, they have. The genius of Jobs, Bill Gates, and others in the computer revolution is that they saw the needs of people and created systems, programs, and products to meet those needs. They didn't expect people to conform to their set-in-stone product line. Instead, they constantly adapted their products to meet the needs of the users.

Christian leaders need the same kind of single-minded focus and willingness to do whatever it takes, not for a state-of-the-art computer on a desktop, but for Jesus Christ himself.

Christian leaders need the same kind of single-minded focus and willingness to do whatever it takes, not for a state-of-the-art computer on a desktop, but for

Jesus Christ himself. We have the most revolutionary message the world has ever known. And while we should never dilute the message of the gospel in order to be more relevant, we need to adapt our methods to get that message to people so we will become "all things to all men so that by all means we may save some." Pastorpreneurs will lead the church to embrace entrepreneurial strategies to reach people without compromising the message. Entrepreneurs will come alongside pastors and church leaders to help change the world around them.

Needs are met in the context of community. Even Christ, the one who possesses all power and authority, didn't minister alone. He called twelve men to follow him so they could emulate his example and soak up his character. In his letter to the Galatians, Paul wrote, "Carry each other's burdens, and in this way you will fulfill the law of Christ. . . . For each one should carry his own load" (Gal 6:2,5). The "burden" Paul referred to is like a load of bricks. No one can handle it on his own. The word translated "load," however, refers to a weight much like a backpack. It represents the normal cares and responsibilities that all of us shoulder each day.

At times each of us feels overwhelmed with the burden of heartache, loss, and problems. The crushing weight during those desperate times can be lightened by the care and assistance of others. Then, as we heal and learn and grow, we become capable of taking our eyes off ourselves and helping others. We never condemn anyone for struggling with a burden he can't carry on his own, but we try to put him in the context of a loving community because that's where people experience the most healing and hope.

The community is the environment where God touches lives most often and most deeply. If a Christian leader is hesitant to be involved in a community, he or she has character problems that must be addressed before destruction comes. Isolation breeds pride or depression—or both. All of us, even the most celebrated leaders among us, need the honesty, kindness, and support we find in the love of a group of believers.

Back to the Heart of God

Jesus' parable of the sheep and the goats in Matthew 25 shows us the circular relationship between our experience of the heart of God and our determination to meet the needs of people. The passage tells us:

> "Then the King will say to those on his right [the sheep], 'Come you who are blessed by my Father; take your inheritance, the kingdom prepared for you since the creation of the world. For I was hungry and you gave me something to eat, I was thirsty and you gave me something to drink, I was a stranger and you invited me in, I needed clothes and you clothed me, I was sick and you looked after me, I was in prison and you came to visit me.'
>
> "Then the righteous will answer him, 'Lord, when did we see you hungry and feed you, or thirsty and give you something to drink? When did we see you a stranger and invite you in, or needing clothes and clothe you? When did we see you sick or in prison and go to visit you?'
>
> "The King will reply, 'I tell you the truth, whatever you did for one of the least of these brothers of mine, you did for me' " (Matt 25:34-40).

Our desire to serve comes from our experience of God's heart, his greatness and grace. Then, as we serve, we realize that every single act of service, no matter how small—and indeed, the point in this passage is the importance of seemingly small acts of love—elicits God's heart-felt appreciation.

When we realize Jesus smiles when we serve others, we are again touched deeply by the kindness of God who loves us deeply and tenderly. It is an unspeakable privilege to serve him, and every act of service strengthens the bond of love we enjoy with him.

When we realize Jesus smiles when we serve others, we are again touched deeply by the kindness of God who loves us deeply and tenderly.

"Lord, Give Me a Dream"

Catherine Marshall was a woman of purpose. She and her gifted husband Peter had a profound impact on millions of people through their speaking, writing, and ministering to the top political leaders of our country. But Catherine, like all of us, went through times of doubt and discouragement. Her vision was clouded, her purpose blurred. She refused to stay in that emotional and spiritual quagmire one minute longer than the Lord required. She prayed passionately,

> *Father,*
> *once I had such big dreams, so much anticipation of the future.*
> *Now no shimmering horizon beckons me; my days are lack-lustre*
> *I see so little of lasting value in the daily round. Where is Your plan for my life?*
>
> *You have told us that without vision, we men perish. So, Father in heaven, knowing that I can ask in confidence for what is Your expressed will to give me, I ask You to deposit in my mind and heart that particular dream, the special vision You have for my life.*
>
> *And along with the dream, will You give me whatever graces, patience, and stamina it takes to see the dream through to fruition?*

*I sense this may involve adventures I have not
bargained for.*

*But I want to trust You
    enough to follow even if You lead along new paths.*

*I admit to liking some of my ruts.
But I know that habit patterns
    that seem like cozy nests from the inside,
        from Your vantage point
            may be prison cells.*

*Lord,
    if you have to break down
        any prisons of mine
    before I can see the stars and catch the vision,
        then, Lord, begin the process now.
In joyous expectation.*

Amen.[11]

> **Then the fire of love for God and love for people will burn again, and we will delight in doing whatever it takes to please God, reach people, and build strong leaders.**

Does Catherine Marshall's prayer ring in your own heart? For some of us, our vision has been sandpapered away by constant criticism and stress. For others, that vision was shattered by failure. And for many others, the dream is still there, but it could use a booster shot to reignite the passion and purpose. Then the fire of love for God and love for people will burn again, and we will delight in doing whatever it takes to please God, reach people, and build strong leaders.

---

11 Catherine Marshall, *Adventures in Prayer,* (Chosen Books, Fleming H. Revell Company, 1975).

Change is needed in the church. The process begins with the heart-felt conviction that what *is* ought not to be, and what *can* be could be. Change in individuals and organizations begins with insight into God's compassion for people, and it progresses with the grit, tenacity, and hope that the Yukon miners had for the gold they sought. But our prize is far greater, far higher, far better—the honor of Jesus Christ as he uses us to change lives for eternity. That prize is worth the risk.

Reflection

1. On a scale of 0 (not at all) to 10 (to the max), rate yourself in these three facets of God's calling. Explain your answers.

    ___ Experiencing the heart of God

    ___ Understanding the needs of people around you

    ___ Identifying and using your gifts and abilities

2. Review the reports about unchurched people and the state of discipleship in our churches. How do you feel when you read these? Do you feel compelled to do anything about these needs? If so, what?

3. Why do you think many church leaders don't cry (like Christ did when he saw the needs of people) or laugh more (like Christ probably did when people responded in faith to him)?

4. Describe the significance of a person touching the heart of God and seeing the needs of people.

5. What are some ways you can gather more information about the demographics and needs of people in your community?

6. Read Catherine Marshall's prayer again. Does it reflect your heart's condition right now? If it does, take some time to make her prayer your own.

7. What might take place in your ministry when God answers that prayer?

4 Clarifying the Vision

"Then Jesus came to them and said, 'All authority in heaven and on earth has been given to me. Therefore go and make disciples of all nations, baptizing them in the name of the Father and of the Son and of the Holy Spirit, and teaching them to obey everything I have commanded you. And surely I am with you always, to the very end of the age' " (Matt 28:18-20).

Not Either-Or

The strength of some Christian leaders is shepherding God's people. They care deeply about their flocks and they spend their energies to help them grow. Others focus on reaching the lost. Their hearts are gripped with the reality of eternity, and they orchestrate programs to proclaim the gospel to anyone and everyone. Far too often, leaders have an "either-or" mentality, either shepherding or outreach, but God has called us to both. The Great Commission is the summary purpose statement for the church and for individuals in the church. It begins with an affirmation that Christ is the source of our strength and power, and it ends with his assurance that he is always by our side. Sandwiched between those encouragements are the commands to go, make disciples, baptize, and teach.

When these words were first spoken, the eleven disciples standing on that hill had watched Christ model a lifestyle of trust in the Father, total commitment to the Father's purposes, and patience and persistence while following the Father's ways. Now he was handing the baton to them. Their mission was not to just proclaim the gospel, but to help the converted grow in their faith so they too would become beacons of light in their world. But even if thousands trusted Christ on a single day (which happened a few days later at Pentecost), they weren't to stop proclaiming the gospel in order to focus on nurturing the infant believers.

Those first church leaders had been given a double mission to proclaim and to nurture. Both—not one or the other. These two crucial aspects of ministry were to be held in dynamic tension and complement one another. Our personalities and experiences may nudge us to one side or the other. Some of us feel more comfortable and effective in outreach, and others may see more success in building young believers into strong disciples. A wise leader, however, recognizes his tendencies and makes adjustments so both aspects remain strong.

> *A wise leader, however, recognizes his tendencies and makes adjustments so both aspects remain strong.*

Rick Warren's Top Ten List

I have already mentioned the way God used Rick Warren's *The Purpose Driven Church* to challenge my desire to be safe and get me out of my comfort zone. Rick lists ten statements that help clarify the vision of a person or an organization. These statements blend outreach and discipleship in powerful ways. He calls them his "top ten list."

#10 "A church will never grow beyond its capacity to meet needs."

#9 "Evaluate your church by asking, 'What is our business?' and then, 'How's business?'"

#8 "What really attracts large numbers of the unchurched to a church are changed lives."

#7 "I've discovered that challenging people to a serious commitment actually attracts people rather than repels them."

#6 "I am continually humbled by God's power to use ordinary people in extraordinary ways."

#5 "Jesus never lowered His standards, but He always started where people were."

#4 "Money spent on evangelism is never an expense, it's always an investment."

#3 "Intelligent, caring conversation opens the door for evangelism with non-believers faster than anything else I've used."

#2 "Increasing the size of your church is simple; you must get more people to visit."

#1 "If you will concentrate on building people, God will build the church."[12]

These statements are tremendously helpful to keep us from drifting into an "either-or" mentality and staying in our comfort zones instead of living in dynamic tension between outreach and discipleship. At our church we try hard to maintain this balance.

The next five chapters describe five strategies from my own life and our church's experience. As you will see, each of these strategies connects the two parts of ministry, evangelism and nurture. Instead of isolating evangelistic programs and discipleship programs, and then trying to balance them, these strategies blend them into a powerful, complementary force to build God's kingdom. We have tried to be entrepreneurial at each step of the way to respond to the call of God to change our community for his glory.

---

12 Rick Warren, *The Purpose Driven Church*, (Zondervan Publishing, Grand Rapids, Michigan).

Introducing the Five Strategies

Before we dive into each of these strategies in detail, I want to briefly introduce them.

Strategy #1 Grab the Community's Attention

The church seems irrelevant to many people in our communities today. Most of them simply will not come to us, so we have to go to them. When we step into their world, we want to be attractive, relevant, and positive—which will elicit the same responses of curiosity and faith as those who listened when Jesus went to them.

Many churches plan virtually all of their activities and spend all of their resources on the "insiders." Others have discovered that by providing selfless services for their communities, many "outsiders" will quickly respond. One church is known for building and renovating homes for the poor, another has incredible musical programs, and another is known for its program to help the unemployed find jobs. The list of services and entertainment a church can provide in the name of Christ is almost endless. These are an open door for your people to reach out in attractive, powerful ways to those in their neighborhoods.

> *Others have discovered that by providing selfless services for their communities, many "outsiders" will quickly respond.*

As it is in most towns and cities, the Fourth of July is a big deal in Carson Valley. When we arrived, the only public place to celebrate that day was at a park that cost about $35 for a family to attend. The leaders of our church saw this as an opportunity to have our own celebration, meet people, and develop a positive impression on hundreds who don't go to church. For the next Fourth, we put an ad in the local newspaper, grilled hot dogs, printed t-shirts, and had all kinds of activities for every age. In response, we had about 2000 people on our grounds! That's two percent of the population of our area, so we were thrilled. The heart-felt appreciation of those who attended was even more significant than the number who came. A number of people tried to give us money to defray the cost, but we refused to take any. Several moms had tears in their eyes as they thanked us for providing such a positive place for their children that day. Our event certainly grabbed the community's attention—and became an annual affair.

Strategy #2 Build Strategic Partnerships

Our Fourth of July event is a perfect example of building strategic partnerships that benefit all involved. Before our second event, I talked to a man in our church who owns a grocery store. I told him, "We want to grill hot dogs for people, and we don't want to charge them anything because it's an outreach. The problem is that we need to keep the costs down. Could you help us with the food costs? We'll put a sign up that says the food was donated by your store." He agreed (but he would not let us put up a sign), and even donated all the food for the entire event. His generosity was a great help to us, and the opportunity to give proved to be a wonderful blessing for him.

Strategy #3 Conduct Faith-Building Events

We try to plan every event so that it challenges, encourages, and stimulates the faith of those who attend as well as those who plan and host it. We don't just have events and hope these purposes are fulfilled. It is the goal and intent of everything we do. Some of our events are held off-site, such as a yearly baptism at Lake

We don't just have events and hope these purposes are fulfilled. It is the goal and intent of everything we do.

Tahoe about 12 miles from our church, and some are out-reach events like the Fourth of July. We also include events that are perceived as our regular events but are given special significance, such as our "40 Days of Purpose" when our worship services focus on particular passages from the Scriptures about living according to God's divine purposes.

Not long ago, we gave $10 to people who attended our worship service and we told them, "In the next thirty days, multiply this money and use it to the glory of God. You can use it any way you wish, as long as it is honoring to the Lord." (I was afraid some people might go to the casino and put the money on red at the roulette table, but to my knowledge, nobody did that!) Some people gave it away to a needy person that same afternoon, and others invested the money so they would have more to give away at the end of the month. One lady used the money to buy supplies for a craft project. She sold the finished product, and used the proceeds to buy more supplies to make even more crafts. By the end of that month, she had made a considerable amount of money to give toward the needs of others. She was thrilled!

Strategy #4 Every Person is a 10—Get 'Em Moving!

Every person has a role or a place where he serves most gladly and most effectively. It is the task of leadership to help people find that place. In a volunteer organization like the church, the payoff isn't money. It's the feeling that, "I made a difference in someone's life." And that's worth everything.

Our church's training program for believers helps people understand the compelling motivation of the love of God, and then encourages them to find a role in which they feel excited and fulfilled. We never try to fill slots by using guilt to get someone to serve. Any short-term gains would be offset by long-term devastating losses—for the person, for the church, and for the leader who tried that heavy-handed, manipulative tactic. I love to see the joy in people's eyes when they see God use them in others' lives.

Strategy #5 Multiply Your Impact

Every person is an apprentice of someone else, and eventually, everyone can be a mentor to another person. It's not enough just to be a good teacher, greeter, evangelist, leader, giver, or servant. God's blueprint for personal and organizational growth is that we multiply our character and our skills in the lives of others. Paul wrote to Timothy, "And the things you have heard me say in the presence of many witnesses entrust to reliable men who will also be qualified to teach others" (II Tim 2:2).

God hasn't called us to be Lone Rangers. Instead, he wants us to use our skills in mentoring relationships so others are touched and want to emulate our skills. *Individuals* multiply their impact by mentoring others. *Churches* multiply their impact by planting new churches, resurrecting dying ones, and sending out missionaries.

> **Individuals** *multiply their impact by mentoring others.* **Churches** *multiply their impact by planting new churches, resurrecting dying ones, and sending out missionaries.*

The Case for Change

In the first three chapters, we addressed the need for organizational change to meet the critical needs in our communities and make sure we present the gospel of Christ in powerful, relevant ways. In this section, I want to address the need for personal change. This change occurs in three areas: the development of skills, tools, and networks.

Skills

The most important skills a Christian leader can develop are the issues we've already addressed: his grasp of God's heart of compassion and strength, being gripped with the needs of people in his community, and an accurate assessment and use of the abilities God has entrusted to him. As these skills develop, the leader will increasingly trust God's sovereign will, weep with the lost and hurting, and stay motivated to use every ounce of his abilities for the glory of God. This is a dynamic, learning, growing process—one that doesn't end in this life.

Peter Senge, author of *The Fifth Discipline,* wrote: "Any organization that intends to grow must be a learning organization." Those who have a passion for learning usually realize they are deficient in some area. That sense of need drives them to read, to study, and to ask questions. They aren't satisfied with things the way they are, and they long to learn so they can fill the gaps in their own understanding. Their goal is not knowledge for the sake of knowledge. Rather, knowledge becomes a tool to accomplish change.

In his outstanding book, *7 Habits of Highly Effective People,* Steven Covey wrote of the necessity of "sharpening your saw," keeping an edge mentally, emotionally, spiritually, and relationally so we don't become dull and ineffective. Almost three millennia ago, Solomon wrote, "If the ax is dull and its edge unsharpened, more strength is needed but skill will bring success" (Ecc 10:10).

When a lumberjack or carpenter notices that his saw isn't cutting well, he has a choice to make. He can keep cutting with the increasingly dull blade, and he will have to expend more effort and take more time to get the job done. Or he can stop for a few minutes, take out his file, and focus his attention on making his saw sharper and more effective. Has he wasted these minutes filing his saw? He certainly hasn't cut any wood during that time, but those minutes are an investment that pays great dividends in time and effort over the next hour or so.

Some of us became dull months or years ago. In fact, it's been so long that we don't even know where to look for the file! But we need to find one and do whatever it takes to become sharp again. "Sharp" people are excited about God's calling. They have read the latest articles and books, and they are eager to share what they are learning. Sharpened leaders are eager to try new things, and their enthusiasm is infectious to those around them. These leaders have learned to value the file as much as the saw because it makes them far more effective. Entrepreneurs must keep growing and learning or else they won't stay on the cutting edge very long.

Tools

The second area of personal change is to develop tools that help us meet the needs of people in our communities. These tools may be specific strategies like the ones in this book, or they may be curricula for classes or groups. A fresh, new system of communication is a tool in the hands of someone who wants to communicate vision and encouragement. Many churches effectively use the Internet and email to get information to key leaders or to send prayer requests to many people as quickly as possible.

When I go to a conference, I ask pastors to tell me the very best things they have done in the past year, the things that have accomplished the most in their ministries. Some of them tell me about a new

When I go to a conference, I ask pastors to tell me the very best things they have done in the past year, the things that have accomplished the most in their ministries.

way of reaching people with the gospel that touched many people who had never responded before. Some talk about a powerful retreat with their leaders, or perhaps a retreat they took just to refresh themselves.

When I hear all kinds of things that these leaders have tried, sometimes I think, "That's a great idea! Why didn't I think of that?" I can implement some of their suggestions immediately. Other ideas don't fit our church for some reason or another, but perhaps I can get a seed of an idea from that person's experience that will germinate into something completely different in our church.

Some leaders try to implement strategies and tools that have worked for a particular church without understanding the context. They expect to start a church in a theater and have a Willow Creek spring up in a few months! It is essential to take time to ask questions about leadership, timing, and communication as you listen to people. When you go to conferences, ask the hard questions about how a strategy applies in certain situations, and how their leaders responded each step of the way. And be sure to ask about the hard decisions and the cost at each step.

Sometimes we look at churches such as Willow Creek or Windsor Hills United Methodist as they are today, and we don't see the hard work, discipline, and crises of faith that got them to this point. Every successful leader and successful church has faced times of testing and trouble. These leaders had the courage to ask good questions, seek God's answers, and take risks. As you read the rest of this book about the strategies that you and your church can implement, be sure to ask those same hard questions.

Networks

The third essential element for change is to develop powerful networks. The motto of our church is "Friends

Helping Friends Follow Christ." Everything we do is in the context of relationships.

Jesus was God in the flesh. He was immutable and self-sufficient, but he still took people with him to accomplish the Father's will. Each of us needs encouragement (often) and rebuke (sometimes), but we miss out on both unless we're around someone who cares about us. Networks form a web of encouragement that moves in all directions, up the lines of authority, laterally to friends and peers in ministry, and down to those we shepherd. Following the example of Timothy, each of us needs an authority figure to guide us, like Paul, someone like Titus or others Paul mentored as a trusted friend and compatriot, and a few "faithful men" to pour our lives into.

Steve Wilson, our Pastor of Spiritual Growth at Carson Valley Christian Center, is a very bright man who earned a degree in social ecology, the study of the relationship between people and their environments. Steve responded to God's call to the pastorate, but he realized in seminary and in his ministry experiences that his chief calling is not in platform speaking. Those who minister with him, however, realize that he has incredibly keen insights into the process of spiritual growth. He understands how people learn and respond to God, and he is brilliant at developing and orchestrating systems and relationships that help people take steps in this process.

Steve is able to comprehend large and complex bodies of information, to design systems that help people grasp that information and take specific steps of growth, and then to work with a leadership team which implements these tools in the lives of hundreds of lives. One of the positive effects Steve has had on our body of believers is that everybody can see that you don't have to be an extrovert or a platform speaker to be used by God. This reality has encouraged a huge number of people and opened wide doors of ministry to them. Steve is an excellent example of someone who developed his skills and continually sharpens his saw.

Steve has found the "sweet spot" of his life where his efforts are having the maximum impact and he is most fulfilled.

I used to play tennis, and I learned that a racket has a "sweet spot" in the center. If the ball hits the strings there, it flies truer and faster than any other place on the face of the racket. Steve has found the "sweet spot" of his life where his efforts are having the maximum impact and he is most fulfilled. That's what happens when each of us, no matter what our specific leadership role may be, realizes our need to grow and develops essential skills, tools, and networks.

Janell Sheets is a very gifted schoolteacher who is on the other end of the introvert-extrovert spectrum. She has taken part in our STEP (Striving to Experience Peace) ministry for emotionally and spiritually wounded people. Her honesty about her own struggles has given her a wonderful, powerful ministry that she never dreamed she could have when she hid those hurts in her own life. In those earlier years, she was highly effective as a teacher, but now her effectiveness is combined with depth of insight and warmth, and God has given her a place of ministry to capitalize on her skills, tools, and networks of relationships.

Steve and Janell are excellent examples of our church's three core values which find expression in their development and use of skills, tools, and networks. These values are:
- People matter to God,
- God's word changes lives, and
- Spiritual growth happens in community.

Identifying and developing those essential elements is not always clear, clean, and simple. Sometimes we learn more through failure than we learn through success. There are many high performance people who hydroplane through life, moving quickly but only skimming the surface, but hydroplaning is not the abundant life Christ offers. In fact, the drive to accomplish great goals may be a hindrance to God's work in our lives. He works most powerfully when we are honest enough to admit our needs.

There are many high performance people who hydroplane through life, moving quickly but only skimming the surface, but hydroplaning is not the abundant life Christ offers.

Quite often in the mystery of God's will, the dark threads of pain and heartache seem to blot out the lighter colored threads of joy and love. For a while, all we see is the backside of the tapestry. Someday—perhaps tomorrow, perhaps not until we see the Lord face to face—we will see the front side of the fabric in all its complexity and beauty. We will see that the dark threads of failure and hurt are woven into our joys in such a way that we are thrilled with the depth, richness, and vibrancy of God's work in our lives. Today, though, we need faith to believe that God is using our pain, our deficiencies, and our struggles to create something beautiful.

Reflection

1. What are some reasons it is easier to be *either* outreach focused or discipleship focused instead of blending the two into a powerful synergy?

2. Would you say your leadership and your church blends these two fairly well, or would you define it as "either-or"? Explain.

3. Look at Rick Warren's "Top Ten List." Which of his statements stand out to you? Why?

   Which statements do you need to focus on to find better balance in your leadership? Explain.

4. Who are some good examples of people you know who have developed . . .
   . . . essential skills of leadership (according to this chapter's explanation)?

   . . . essential tools of leadership?

   . . . essential networks in leadership?

chapter 5

Strategy #1: Grab the Community's Attention

"Then he said to his disciples, 'The harvest is plentiful but the workers are few. Ask the Lord of the harvest, therefore, to send out workers into his harvest' " (Matt 9:37-38).

The late Sam Shoemaker, an Episcopalian bishop, talked about the type of "outreach" common in many churches today: "In the Great Commission the Lord has called us to be like Peter—fishers of men. We've turned the Commission around so that we have become merely keepers of the aquarium. Occasionally I take some fish out of your fishbowl and put them into mine, and you do the same with my bowl. But we're all tending the same fish."[13]

Christians have many problems that cry out for attention—real hurts and desperate needs. And it's easy for a church to become so absorbed by its own members' needs that it has little if any time to devote to the needs of those outside its walls. Instead of putting energy and creativity into reaching beyond our "fishbowls," we have resorted to fish swapping. We end up with different fish than we had before, so we tell ourselves that we are making a difference.

Another problem churches experience in their attempts to connect with our culture is that young believers often

---

13 Em Griffin, *The Mindchangers*, (Tyndale House, 1976), p. 151.

> *It means that all of us . . . are called by God to live holy and pure lives and to maintain meaningful contact with lost people so we can truly be his ambassadors to them.*

lose touch with their lost friends. Various studies show that two to three years after a person trusts Christ, he has grown in his faith so that he has new values and a new lifestyle. In addition, he has developed a new circle of friends, the ones with whom he worships, goes to Bible studies, and calls for advice. In those two or three years, he effectively changes his social orbit and loses his connections with his former friends, who are primarily lost people.

In Jesus priestly prayer, he prays for us because we live in a dynamic tension: We are *in the world* (John 17:11) but *not of the world* (17:6). What does that mean? It means that all of us, from young Christians to those who have been in the faith for decades, are called by God to live holy and pure lives *and* to maintain meaningful contact with lost people so we can truly be his ambassadors to them.

Stay Connected Personally

Most church leaders can easily spend all their time absorbed in the matters of church business: studying for sermons or classes, preparing for meetings, helping church members through difficulties in their lives, calling the repair service to fix the copier, and all manner of things that eat their time and energies. Those things need attention, but they shouldn't absorb *all* our time.

One of the critical responsibilities of Christian leadership is to get connected and stay connected to people in our neighborhoods. To be "in the world," we can strike up conversations with people about all kinds of things that interest them—not just spiritual stuff. We can develop relationships with people who contribute nothing to our church goals or our personal goals . . . just because we care enough to carve out time for them. How many of us have friends—real friends—who aren't connected with our church . . . or any church? When the time is right, we can turn conversations to Christ—not to put another notch on our spiritual gun belt, but to share the life-transforming love of Christ with a new friend.

Let's be honest. We have plenty of pressures to stay in our "holy huddles." We experience the pressure of habit and the pressure of inertia. We have developed patterns of life that have gradually shifted to church friends and church responsibilities, away from meaningful contact with unbelievers. We now feel much more comfortable doing what we've always done with the people who believe the way we do.

We also endure the pressure of expectations. The people in our churches expect us to spend our time and energies on them. They have needs, they contribute the church, and they expect us to jump when they need us. When we're out building relationships with unbelievers, there's a little less time to do what we've done before to meet the needs of our flock. Is the shift worth it?

Dallas Theological Seminary professor Howard Hendricks is widely quoted as saying, "If you want people to bleed, you have to hemorrhage." We can't expect those around us to care for the lost if they don't see us deeply moved by the realities of heaven and hell. They are not only listening to our words; they are watching our actions. In fact, they are watching to see that our actions match our words. That's what builds or destroys our credibility.

Followers typically do a bit less than their leaders. One person called this phenomenon a "negative one differential factor." What do people see us doing? Whatever it is, they will do a little less. If they know I'm sharing Christ with two

What do people see us doing? Whatever it is, they will do a little less.

neighbors, they will share the gospel with one of theirs. If I make time to go to my children's sporting events and use that time to develop rich, real relationships with other parents, those who follow me may have the courage to at least start conversations with unchurched people.

This admonition to set a good example is not meant to be a guilt trip. I look in the mirror whenever I say or write things like this. I have to ask myself, "Am I on the cutting edge, or am I slipping toward the holy huddle? Do I carve out time to regularly relate to unbelievers? And when I do, do they see me as a friend or as someone who's trying to manipulate them to do what I want them to do?"

Stay Connected Organizationally

You probably will notice that as we address the five strategies, they fit together with powerful synergy for maximum impact. They can be implemented individually, but they are meant to form a cohesive whole that affects people inside and outside the church. Big events, partnerships, leadership development, and multiplying our effectiveness work together to nurture young believers, build strong leaders, and reach out to everyone in your community. Strategies and structures are designed, then, to accomplish multiple goals. All this begins, though, with eyes to see the purposes of God and the lostness of people around us.

I am always moved by Matthew's account of Jesus' grassroots ministry, compassionate heart, and clear call:

"Jesus went through all the towns and villages, teaching in their synagogues, preaching the good news of the kingdom and healing every disease and sickness. When he saw the crowds, he had compassion on them, because they were harassed and helpless, like sheep without a shepherd. Then he said to his disciples, 'The harvest is plentiful but the workers are few. Ask the Lord of the harvest, therefore, to send out workers into his harvest' " (Matt 9:35-38).

The role of spiritual leadership is to model a life of compassion and activism, to communicate the gospel to people who come to church to hear it and to take it those who don't come to you. As leaders model the ministry of Christ, they prepare workers to communicate the grace of God with power, clarity, and kindness. In all of this, the equipping of workers is to instill them with a strong sense of hope that the message of Christ changes lives.

> *The role of spiritual leadership is to model a life of compassion and activism. . . .*

I've known people who shared the gospel primarily because they believed it was the right thing to do. They saw some results, but not many. And I've known other men and women who were so gripped with the grace of God themselves that they couldn't imagine anyone saying "no" to Christ. They saw the fields as "plentiful" and ripe, and in response, many trusted Christ. In addition, the enthusiasm of these faith-filled workers inspired dozens more with the compelling desire to share their faith, and the workers multiplied. Our expectations make a world of difference.

Again, maintaining high expectations begins with seeing the unseen, looking past someone's expensive car and fat bank account to observe an empty heart. Jesus "saw the crowds," but not just their faces and numbers. He saw the condition of their hearts, and his own heart broke for them.

One of the finest books on discipleship ever written is called *Master Plan of Evangelism,* by Robert Coleman. It describes how God's method of evangelizing the world is to build disciples who have his heart for the lost. Their commitment to sharing the gospel heightens disciples' dependence on Christ, sharpens their study of the Scriptures, and enriches their relationships with other disciples who are "in the battle with them" as well as with unbelievers who become their friends.

Preparing disciples doesn't happen by accident. It requires intention, planning, modeling, celebrating successes, and the willingness to ask hard questions. A cardinal rule of communication is: "Know your audience." That rule is certainly true in connecting with people in our communities.

In one of his online articles, George Barna asked helpful questions: "Does your congregation know how to connect with the unchurched? Has time been spent evaluating the attitudes, goals, belief systems and church expectations of the unchurched? Once you have an understanding of where the unchurched are coming from, you will have a clear picture of how to meet them where they are."[14]

When we have a clear picture of the demographics and needs in our neighborhoods, we can implement a strategy to *attract* people to Christ, *attach* them to people in the church, and *activate* them as coworkers in the harvest.

Attract

Flyfishermen are students of "the hatch" in a stream. They carefully examine the insects on top of the water and the nymphs and larvae under rocks and in the currents. After they know what type of insect the trout are eating, they choose the right fly. Careful analysis is essential, or they won't catch fish.

---

14 ConnectingPoint 03.11.2003, Pastorsline.com

Careful analysis is just as important if "fishers of men" want to be successful. The United States Census Bureau (go to http://factfinder.census.gov/servlet/AGSGeoAddress Servlet?_lang=en&_programYear=50&_treeId=420 and enter a street address for some wonderful resources!) and most denominational headquarters provide excellent demographic information so you can review the existing make-up of your community and the trends over the past few years. This information is vitally important to help you understand the people to whom God has called you to minister. In addition, conduct your own informal interviews with people to discover what is important to different groups in the area. Sports, music, children's programs, finances, and marriage are almost universally important issues, but as you study your community, there may be particular angles on these topics or others that come to light. These needs and interests become open doors to grab people's attention.

New Hope Community Church in Oceanside, California, wanted to attract the media-saturated and culturally sophisticated community in the San Diego area. Scott Evans, an associate pastor at the church, had a marketing background. He designed creative brochures, direct mail pieces, door hangers, water bottles, and all kinds of other tools to get the word out about the church. He first urged the leaders of the church to establish a clear, strong sense of identity. He then communicated that identity in every tool he created. A church's identity reflects its grasp of God's purposes and character, and how God wants to use the gifted people in the church to meet the specific needs of people in that community.

When we came to Carson Valley, we talked to scores of people to find out what they wanted and needed. We found that many of them felt a lot of stress about their teenage kids, so one of the first newspaper inserts we developed and one of the first sermons I preached was "Raising G-Rated

The point was to identify a basic need and provide an answer to meet that need.

Kids in an X-Rated World." The point was to identify a basic need and provide an answer to meet that need. In fact, the topic of every sermon at our church is designed to address a specific need, and our marketing pieces are created to raise public awareness of our attempts to do so.

Establishing your church's identity is extremely important. It becomes the motto or tagline that people associate with your church. This identity is not determined by democratic vote. It is the responsibility of those who have been entrusted with the vision God has given the church. In a church plant like Carson Valley five years ago, our identity came from our sense of God's passion and power, the specific needs of people in this area, and the unique blend of gifts and passions of the church leaders. Through a lot of prayer and discussion, God gave us a clear sense of identity: "Friends Helping Friends Follow Christ." That certainly isn't all we are, but it's the core of what we hope to be.

We believe that effective ministry takes place within relationships through the power and grace of Jesus Christ. In existing organizations, entrenchment and inertia are normal. Change comes hard. The pastor has to earn the right to gather the key leaders of the church to determine a clear, and perhaps new, identity. A visionary leader is wise to take time to build relationships and win respect and trust before he attempts to change course.

John Kotter, a Harvard professor who is an expert in analyzing change processes, says people must first realize the compelling need for change in order for change to take place. In a church, the pastor has to create the awareness that change is needed. If the leader establishes his credibility and wins people's trust, he will overcome normal obstacles, or at least minimize them. Otherwise, he can expect inevitable roadblocks, foot-dragging, and conflicts.

To earn a hearing, a pastor has to point the congregation patiently and persistently to God's heart and people's needs. He has to show them that what exists isn't all that God wants for them and their community. The pastor's role as a visionary, then, is to introduce "disequalibrium," the sense that change is necessary. He has to overcome inertia and lack of vision with the faith and confidence that God can do far more.

Don't read this book or come home from a conference and single-handedly declare your church's new identity. That would be vocational suicide! The process of determining an organization's identity often takes months as you conduct research to identify needs, fine-tune the sense of God's calling, and win respect. Take your time. Patience will pay off in clarity, consistency, and more unity than you would have otherwise. Of course, no matter what you do, there will be some who always feel that change is wrong. They are wedded to the traditions of generations past or the leaders of yesterday. Be gracious to them, but don't stop the boat because a few don't want to get on.

The commitment to attract people gives us a reason to be creative, to think outside the box. Hold events off-campus occasionally to make it easier for unbelievers to feel comfortable. Target segments of the community who have been neglected for years, perhaps the down-and-outers or the up-and-outers. Focus attention on the unemployed or single moms. Do whatever will make a positive difference in your neighborhood. Creative thinking and planning unleashes the wealth of resources in the church to touch lives in the community, and it stimulates the faith and excitement of church members God uses to touch those people.

> *Warmth and a powerful message of hope will attract people, but we also need to identify and avoid the things that definitely repel them.*

Warmth and a powerful message of hope will attract people, but we also need to identify and avoid the things that definitely repel them. Bickering among church members is one of the most harmful (and all too common) problems. One newspaper account reported a fistfight at a church's business meeting as they talked about the budget for the next year. Wouldn't you like to hear about the love of Christ from that crowd? When unbelievers hear about one believer slamming another believer at work or in the neighborhood, who can blame them for not getting involved in those people's churches?

Another turnoff for many people is an overemphasis on money. Stewardship is one of our church's 10 core values, but using guilt to get people to give certainly isn't. Jesus talked more about money than he talked about prayer and faith combined, but never to twist someone's arm to give. When money has become an obstacle to faith or even an idol, the problem needs to be addressed to help people experience God's goodness and grace more fully. Communicate often and always: "God loves a cheerful giver." But giving should always be a response of gratitude for God's grace, not an opportunity to use guilt to meet the church's budget.

Two other turnoffs for the community are a church's irrelevance and poor programming. When we don't offer programs to meet needs and stimulate faith, or when our programs fail to meet anyone's standard of excellence, people walk away. I've seen some children's ministries that were poorly supervised and unsafe for kids. Loving parents would think twice about bringing a child back into that environment, no matter how many times they are invited.

Sometimes your best efforts to promote your church may even provide the community with a source of comic relief. During the first 15 months after our church's launch, we were at a temporary site, so we had to put up a huge vinyl sign each weekend—12 feet by 12 feet, on 16-foot posts beside a major highway. Each Friday afternoon (to put it up) and each Sunday afternoon (to take it down), my brother, his family, three or four other guys, and I gathered beside the road. Whoever was feeling brave that day would climb an eight-foot ladder, stand on the top of it, and either affix or undo zip ties. This was difficult enough under the best of circumstances, but Carson Valley is known for its wind. Sometimes it blew 60 miles an hour, creating a "sail effect" with the vinyl sign. Cars would even stop to cheer us on (or laugh at us). At least we had some shared experiences and a few laughs out of our weekly ordeal—and to be honest, after five years, occasionally we still do crazy things like that!

Attach

Studies show that any organization, and specifically a church, has only a few weeks to help newcomers begin meaningful relationships. Beyond that, visitors feel that relationships are not valued.

Our church wanted to create a welcoming, warm moment as soon as people walk in the doors of our church or come to any of our events, so we created the "First Touch" ministry. Every person is greeted at the door and offered some refreshments. Food is a wonderful way to break the ice and show we care, so we have refreshments at every service and every event.

Our Saturday evening services are preceded by a light meal, and our Sunday worship services offer donuts, juice, and coffee. This created something of a crisis point not long after we moved into our new worship center. Our standing rule (one of the Ten Commandments of churches throughout the world) had been that people could have refreshments in the lobby, but not in the worship service. After about three months, our leaders realized we were teaching people that certain *rooms* were somehow sacred. Instead, we wanted to say that God is sacred, but our stuff is not. So we began to let people bring refreshments into the auditorium. If they spill something, so be it. They have felt more comfortable, and that hasn't been a bad tradeoff.

I believe people ask two inherent questions: "What's in this for me?" and, "Is there anybody here like me?"

Every church has a "stickiness quotient"—factors that determine how easily and how quickly a person can find meaningful relationships after they walk in the door. I believe people ask two inherent questions: "What's in this for me?" and, "Is there anybody here like me?"

The first question addresses their concern about finding something relevant and meaningful to address the needs in their lives. We must be careful not to always assume that those who have needs are poor or outcasts. People at all levels of society need to figure out how to fulfill a dream, find meaning when all their efforts have left them empty, or put a relationship back together.

The second question focuses on feeling connected to people like them. Single moms want to know that they can relate to other single moms, not just married people. Kids want to hang out with kids who have similar interests. Common backgrounds and common needs give people a sense of comfort.

To make sure these questions are addressed, we often include a testimony in our worship services from people who felt nervous when they first attended, but soon connected with a person, a class, or some group in the church. Betsy Kennedy is a single mom who had lived in this area for eight years and had stopped going to church after she and her husband got a divorce. She responded to one of the church's inserts in our local newspaper, and she came to one of our services. At first, she didn't know many people, but soon she met a few more single moms. Their common circumstances and common needs formed a strong bond among them. Betsy soon volunteered to be in charge of our ministry to single moms, and she is having a wonderful impact on mothers and kids today. Although she first attended with a measure of fear, the relationships she established here became, as she would tell you, a true family for her.

Some people refuse to attach in meaningful ways by their own choice. They may be deeply hurt and unwilling to risk connecting again, or they may be hiding something. We tell people they are perfectly welcome to attend and remain anonymous as long as they want, but we don't recommend it. We much prefer that people experience the health God provides by his grace and by his gracious people—health that comes from the warmth and honesty of rich relationships.

Occasionally we must take the blame when people find it difficult to attach to our church. Sometimes we are busy conducting programs and become too absorbed to notice the critical moments when people decide to stay or walk away. Another mistake some leaders make is to over-spiritualize their ministries. They believe, "If God wants visitors to stay, he'll put it in their hearts. If not, then they weren't meant to be here." That sounds very pastoral, but it is an abdication of the role of a shepherd to "know well the state of your flocks" so we can meet their needs.

Many church leaders observe that few newcomers keep coming back, and their conclusion is, "It's their fault.

They're not committed to Christ." Instead, we need to ask the missiological question: "What barriers can we remove to make it easier for people to say 'yes' to Christ and to discipleship?" If missionaries portray the Christian faith as white people listening to hymns played on the organ and the pastor wearing black robes, they have erected barriers which prevent much of the world from understanding the message of Christ. In the same way, I need to remove any and every barrier so that people don't miss the real Jesus. If I have done that, and they still reject Christ, my hands are clean even though my heart will be broken.

Before Haddon Robinson retired from his position at Denver Conservative Baptist Seminary, he wanted every person who got a graduate degree from that school to be trained in missiology. We now live in a post-Christian culture, so every pastor and every church leader in America today is a missionary. But Barna has observed that the church in North America is not as missiological on its home turf as it is when it sends people across oceans. The mindset of global missions, then, needs to be brought home and domesticated to reach people in our communities.

Activate

The task of the church begins with attracting unbelievers by grabbing their attention and then attaching them with warm and affirming relationships. It continues by activating the church members to be involved in this endeavor and the newcomers by integrating them into the life of the body.

Activating people is helping them uncover their gifts and passions so they serve gladly and effectively, and so the light of hope and the fire of desire to please God shine in them. Paul compared each person in a dynamic church with parts of the human body. If each one is healthy and functions well, the body grows strong. But if even a small part is wounded, the entire body suffers. He wrote: "From [Christ] the whole body, joined and held together by every supporting ligament, grows and builds itself up in love, as each part does its work" (Eph 4:16).

Every person plays a vital role in the life of the church. Some play visible roles, and some serve behind the scenes. Some are eyes, some are hands, some are internal organs, and some are toenails. But even the toenail is vitally important. It doesn't command much attention on most days, but have you ever had an ingrown toenail? If so, then you know how much the rest of the body can suffer when even one small part is hurting and out of service.

Activating people is helping them uncover their gifts and passions so they serve gladly and effectively, and so the light of hope and the fire of desire to please God shine in them.

A church cannot grab the community's attention very well if only a handful of people are working like crazy while the rest sit on their hands. We've already addressed why so many people remain inactive. For some reason, they haven't been overwhelmed with the incredible love and power of God. They haven't tapped into his heart, for themselves or for the world. Without this compelling, delightful passion, they are self-absorbed instead of seeing the needs of others. They may come to church and may even be involved on teams or committees, but they lack light and fire.

Let me put it this way: You can send those who don't have this passion to all kinds of classes, seminars, and conferences, and not much will happen until God lights that fire in them. But those who have this fire will seek opportunities all day every day to be used by the Lord they love in the lives of others. And they will be thrilled whenever God shows himself faithful to touch a life through them.

As we've said before, the connection between passion, understanding needs, and discovering spiritual gifts is not linear. It is a dynamic process in which each of these elements is deepened and enriched by hands-on experience. Successes and failures shape our convictions, deepen our dependence on Christ, and clarify the direction of our specific role in the body of Christ.

At Carson Valley Christian Center, the goal of our leadership team is not to fill up an organizational chart. We tell people that most of them will find ministry roles outside the church. We believe people can serve God powerfully in their shop, office, or neighborhood. Being a spiritual leader doesn't mean having your name on a chart. It means finding the passion, place, and people where God calls you to minister, and imparting the love of God with all your heart.

Before he moved away, one member of our congregation was president of the Chamber of Commerce and a member of the City Planning Commission. God gave him an incredible platform for ministry with business leaders. What a shame it would have been if we had muscled him into some slot on an organizational chart and caused him to miss the fantastic opportunities to touch lives where he worked every day. His position as an ambassador for Christ at the Chamber and on the Commission had far more impact than in a "normal" role at our church.

Ray Bakke, a brilliant urban missiologist, reported that the most effective evangelism with Japanese people a few years ago occurred, not in Tokyo or Yokohama, but in Huntsville, Alabama. A Japanese automaker opened a plant in Huntsville, and some of the top executives and engineers came from their home office to spend a year in America. God gave a church in Huntsville a vision for how they could have a global impact for Christ by building relationships and sharing Christ with those execs and engineers. That year four top leaders of the automotive company trusted Christ and went back to Japan as ambassadors for Christ.

Japan is known as a tough place to share the gospel, as many missionaries will tell you. But one American church found a different way to accomplish their mission, and now there are four Japanese business leaders who are standing up for Jesus Christ in Japan. The people in that Huntsville church didn't have "sharing Christ with Japanese business leaders" on their organizational chart, but they went beyond "business as usual" thinking and accomplished something great for God.

Reflection

1. What are some pressures on you to become disconnected from people outside the church (habits, inertia, expectations of others, etc.)?

   What are some specific things you can do to have good conversations and develop friendships with lost people?

2. How does your congregation connect with the unchurched? What is your evaluation of the attitudes, goals, belief systems and church expectations of the unchurched?

3. What principles and specific activities can you implement to *attract* people? When and how do you plan to get started?

4. What are some ways you can tell how people feel when they come to your services or events (without assuming they feel "fine")? How can you do a better job of getting them to *attach*?

5. How does *activating* people relate to grabbing the community's attention?

6. What would it mean for you and your church to think outside the organizational box? How can you encourage people to see opportunities where they live and work as being equally or more important than showing up on the church's organizational chart?

6 Strategy #2: Build Strategic Partnerships

*"Two are better than one,
because they have a good return for their
work" (Ecc 4:9).*

Good battlefield commanders try to marshal all available resources and bring them to bear at the point of attack. Church work isn't as dramatic as combat (with the possible exception of some deacons' meetings I've heard about!), but the principle applies to us, too. Most church leaders overlook a wealth of resources they could use in reaching their communities and building leaders. Those resources are often right under their noses.

When too many good men die in combat, the commanders realize they have to change tactics and find better weapons. In the church, we tend to fight our spiritual battles for the souls of people with the same methods and tools we've used for generations, but the post-Christian, high-tech, Information Revolution has changed the nature of our battle. If we keep fighting in the same ways, we will needlessly lose a lot of people. The comfort of inertia is just not worth the risk of losing so many lives.

Begin with a Vision

Leadership Network has done some great work in helping church leaders think more strategically. In one of their online articles, they address the fact that numerical growth isn't enough. God has called us to make a powerful difference where we live and work. The article states: "More and more congregations are asking the question, 'What difference are we making in our community?' After two decades of increasing their attendance and expanding their facilities, many churches are re-focusing their energies and resources on the transformation of their local communities. This movement has been described as a shift from creating capacity to releasing capacity with the understanding that transformed people transform communities. Within this movement, (one) approach . . . involves a series of alliances and partnerships with other churches, nonprofits, government, and community agencies."[15]

As we have already concluded, change begins with the heartfelt conviction that business as usual isn't making enough of an impact. In our hearts, we believe God wants us to do more, to be more effective, and to realize our people want their lives to count for eternity. We simply aren't satisfied with incremental growth any longer. We have a holy dissatisfaction, a God-given sense that change is not just a good thing; it is absolutely necessary.

We see the faces of those who come to our worship services, and we are thrilled they are there. But what about the thousands and tens of thousands of others nearby whose lives aren't being touched by the Master? How can God use us to bring the dynamic of God's Spirit to their lives? How can our church have a genuine impact on the social fabric of our community? Change begins with us, not those farther down the organizational chart or those working beside us. It begins with me!

---

15 "The Futurity of Present Events," Leadership Network, Christian.washington@leadnet.org

Finding partners and alliances is one way to fulfill the vision God gives us to go farther, do more, and touch more people for his glory. Potential partners are all around us: on Main Street and at City Hall, in our neighborhoods and in our pews, and often sitting in our leadership meetings. As you look for potential partners, you will want relationships that provide shared benefits, and you'll want to work with organizations with shared values. When partnerships are carefully established, they can accelerate the ministry of your church. Solomon wrote of the impact of individuals and organizations working together toward a common goal: "Two are better than one, because they have a good return for their work" (Ecc 4:9).

Shared Benefits

Any good partnership has to work well for both parties, so look for organizations that can also benefit from an alliance with your church. I have already mentioned how a local grocer partnered with us to provide food for our Fourth of July event. This businessman was inspired by the event and wanted to be involved. We thought he would "help out a little" with a few dollars or a few cases of soft drinks. Boy, were we wrong. He donated all the food, all the drinks, and all the eating supplies for the entire event. His generosity saved the church over $4,000! The church did the work to get people there, and we staffed the tables to serve. We wanted to put up a sign that told people his store donated the food, but he wanted to remain anonymous. The benefit he wanted to enjoy was of a different stripe. He experienced the joy of seeing his generosity used by God to accomplish his wonderful purposes. Both of us benefited greatly from this partnership.

A partnership with a government or nonprofit agency can accomplish the purposes of the church and the partner, but you have to watch out for red tape. Be sure to do your homework to find out what is expected and/or required. Government offices are notorious for spending lots of time and energy on a project and then changing their minds. Don't let that be *your* time and energy. On the other side of the ledger, the recent faith-based initiative offers wonderful opportunities to secure funding for programs that can have a profound impact on your community. Find someone with savvy in working with the government. That person can lead the way for you and clear out a lot of potential obstacles.

Shared Values

In most communities, local newspapers are not exactly mouthpieces for evangelical Christianity, but they are always looking for human-interest stories. Whenever we have a particularly interesting speaker or someone to sing or perform at an event, we call the paper and invite them to do a story. We get good promotion in the community, and the paper gets an interesting story to inspire their readers. We have a shared value of touching lives, and we both benefit from the partnership.

Not long ago we hosted a karate expert who was attempting to set the world's record of breaking boards, so we contacted the newspaper and a local television station. On the night of the event, our auditorium was packed. The feeling was electric. The paper's photographer took pictures and the television station filmed the attempt.

In addition to the sporting aspect of this event, the man had been a Hell's Angel who trusted Christ. He was honest about his nagging struggles with some addictive behavior, but his message was strongly Christ-centered and anti-drugs.

The real story that night was not karate; it was that Christ had changed a life. The newspaper and television station were both very happy with the story, and of course, we were glad to get the word out about the transforming grace of God.

Our research in Carson Valley showed us that 80 percent of all households got one of the local papers, so instead of sending mass mailings to people, we put full-color inserts in the local paper. The color inserts were less expensive than an ad in the paper, and they had the added bonus of being separate and could be kept by people long after they had discarded the newspaper.

The newspaper and television station were both very happy with the story, and of course, we were glad to get the word out about the transforming grace of God.

People in every community in the nation are very health-conscious these days, so we asked the local hospital if they would partner with us to conduct a health fair. They were glad to sponsor booths all around our auditorium to give information about a wide range of health-care issues. Why did the hospital participate? Because part of their mission is to inform the community about health-related topics. Why did we sponsor the health fair? Because we know that some people would never come to a worship service, but they would come to our facilities to get free information about their arthritis, gout, cancer, heart disease, diet, or long-term care options. We wanted to remove one more barrier people may have erected to keep them distant from a community of faith. The health fair was a way to connect with them and show we care. This event fit the purposes for both organizations.

Of course, there are some organizations and businesses that we won't partner with. We don't partner with bars or any business with a questionable reputation. We take seriously Paul's admonition to avoid entanglements with the ungodly: "Do not be yoked together with unbelievers. For what do righteousness and wickedness have in common? Or what fellowship can light have with darkness? What harmony is there between Christ and Belial? . . . For we are the temple of the living God" (II Cor 6:14-16).

Make sure any partnership is based on common values, and avoid those that are questionable. For example, if the editor of a local newspaper has a strong, aggressive pro-abortion stance, you will want to have an arms-length relationship with that paper. Find another paper to partner with you, or at least be sure the reporter invited to cover your events provides very positive copy and photos that enhance your church's reputation.

We look for companies and agencies that are already respected in the community. They are the ones that will have the greatest potential for benefiting both them and us by working together.

You don't need to make any long-term commitments with an organization or business. You can keep your arrangements short-term and event-oriented. If it goes well for both of you, the door will be open for the next one. If not, you can walk away without embarrassment or awkwardness.

Finding Good Partners

The Chamber of Commerce can provide good recommendations for partnerships in your local area. As you talk with people in your church, you will hear that this business or that leader has a heart for people and a willingness to help. But don't forget to look for opportunities within your own church and on your own leadership team. Quite often, such people have simply never thought of this kind of partnership, but they would be glad to participate if asked. Entrepreneurs naturally attract other entrepreneurs, so multiply your impact by getting entrepreneurs in your church involved in your vision and strategy.

Not every partnership involves outreach. One master craftsman I know offered to build custom cabinets for every room in the church for what it would cost him in materials. We got about $60,000 worth of gorgeous cabinetry for a fraction of that cost. In the end, we were thrilled, and he was excited that he could use his considerable skills to serve the Lord.

Some organizations are simply waiting for your invitation to partner with them; others have never considered anything like this before. Don't be afraid to brainstorm with your leadership. Think creatively and expansively. A concept that at first seems silly may lead you to another idea that will bear a lot of fruit.

Recently we talked about asking a car dealership to donate a car to be raffled to raise money to provide food for underprivileged families. (We haven't tried this yet, but we're thinking about it.) We could get all kinds of service organizations to help sell tickets, and we could hold the drawing at the car dealership. The media would report the purpose of the event, the progress, and the actual drawing. In the end, the dealership gets terrific publicity, a lot of money is raised to provide food for the hungry, and our church is seen as a compassionate group of people. (Want to buy a ticket?)

When partnering becomes an established habit, you will become more adept at choosing the right organization for a specific event, and you will find those which best match your church's purposes. The selection criteria I use are:

- Identify the laser beam strategy of our purpose for the event and the nature of the partnership.

- Identify the core purpose (worship, evangelism, fellow-ship, discipleship, or service) that this partnership will enhance.
- Identify organizations that are trusted because they have good reputations.
- Identify organizations whose purpose is consistent with ours or is at least complementary to ours.
- Identify organizations that are willing to think outside the box and be as creative as we are.

In some cases, our church will hold the event with or without a partner. A partner would enhance and strengthen the event, but we could get by on our own if necessary. In other cases, however, we simply cannot have a particular event if we don't have a partner or two. The reason may be financial (such as the food at the Fourth of July celebration), or it may be a matter of expertise (as was the case in our health fair).

Creative and Strategic

Sometimes you have to overcome a roadblock or two to make things work. If you're willing to think a little harder, the Lord may accomplish some amazing things.

I have a friend whose community already has a Fourth of July celebration. In fact, his town has hosted an annual parade, concert, and fireworks display for about 50 years. It is one of the most treasured institutions in that town. It would be unwise for my friend's church to sponsor a competing event. However, his church is right in the middle of the parade route. They could pass out bottled water and fans to parade participants, or they could provide lawn chairs and umbrellas for onlookers. The companies that provide the water, fans, chairs, and umbrellas would get good publicity, and the people who sweat through that parade would think this church was heaven-sent!

The timing of an event is very important. When we arrived in Carson Valley, a church at the other end of the valley had held a Harvest Festival on Halloween for years. Their festival was very well run, and many of our people attended it. We didn't see any reason to compete with them, so we were simply participants with them for several years. In time, some people came to us and said, "Their festival is really good, but it's a long way from here. I think it would be good for us to have a Fall Festival at our church." We prayed about it, and we decided to try one of our own. The result is that our festival has become a great success, and the one at the other end of the valley is still going strong.

Every partnership must connect with one of our church's core purposes: evangelism, discipleship, worship, fellowship, and service. We may begin with brainstorming, but we don't go too far before we make sure the event significantly contributes to the purposes and vision the Lord has given us. That perspective is a guiding light in our planning process so we don't lose focus on the reason we hold and promote the event.

> *Every partnership must connect with one of our church's core purposes: evangelism, discipleship, worship, fellowship, and service.*

Every event can mobilize at least some of our leaders and church members to play a part in making it happen. In fact, these partnerships are a good way to get people involved in service for the first time. Every partnership and every event have multiple purposes of outreach, leadership development, and team building.

Seminars have limited success in teaching people about spiritual gifts. They can be helpful and instructive, but most people don't get the light of insight and the fire of desire in their eyes until they are actually involved in a ministry experience. Participation in short-term missions, and by extension, short-term partnership events, are frequently "Aha!" experiences for people who use their abilities for Christ for the first time. In fact, we believe real-life ministry experiences are critical for helping people discover and develop their spiritual gifts for ministry.

Many church leaders are very kind and godly, but they are entrenched in doing the same things in the same ways they have done them for generations. Partnering with organizations in the community gets us out of the rigid box of redundancy and propels us to dream bigger dreams.

A few churches in our area don't like what our church is doing. They see the creative approaches to ministry, and they wonder if we are watering down the gospel or lacing the donuts with some kind of magical magnetism just to get people in the door. Yet while they may not like what we are doing, they will all tell you that we have set a high standard for connecting with the community. We are creative, we are pioneers, and we use any resource we can find to reach out to people. We aren't smarter than anyone else, and we don't have greater abilities than anyone else. But God has given us a vision to take risks to connect with people in fresh ways.

And for the record, we don't water down the gospel at all. We don't try to force the gospel into an event like a health fair. That kind of event is pre-evangelistic—like plowing the fields before the seed is sown. When it's time to sow seeds of the grace of Jesus Christ, we hold nothing back. We do it often, and I trust, we do it well.

Partnerships allow us to do far more than we could possibly accomplish if we had to wait until we raised all the funds to conduct an event. And the payoff is the genuine connections we make with people. When we have 2000 people come to an event, about 1500 of them don't regularly attend our church. That's 1500 fresh, positive impressions on men, women, and children. Some of them may return to worship with us the next week, some may come a few months later when they get a flier about another event we are hosting, and some won't come until they experience a crisis. At that crucial moment in their lives, they may remember, "Those people at that church really cared about me. I could use their help now."

All of us hit bumps in the road. That's the way life is. Partnerships allow us to host more and bigger events so that we can touch additional lives. Perhaps someday, that first touch will pay huge dividends when the person has a spiritual question or a specific need. On that day, when the person is ready, he or she may come to us and discover the warmth, support, and word of Christ.

Partnerships also enable us to have a greater impact with more strategic use of manpower. Our influence is multiplied. The constituency of the hospital aligned themselves with our church for the health fair. We provided some manpower, but our efforts were greatly magnified by the hospital's staff, resources, and reputation in the community.

You may have someone in your church who works for the newspaper, the local cable affiliate, a grocery store, amusement park, car dealership, or print shop. You can begin the process of finding good partners by looking at your current need or looking at the connections of people in your church. Either way, God will lead you to far more resources than you ever imagined, and those partnerships can catapult your church's effectiveness in your community.

A New Way of Thinking

This chapter opened with a quote from Leadership Network about the strategic and creative use of partnerships to meet needs in our communities. Christian Washington, the director of that organization's Missional Church

Network, observes powerful changes in the thinking processes of cutting-edge churches. These churches move:

- From building walls to building bridges in the community.
- From measuring attendance to measuring impact.
- From encouraging saints to attend services to equipping saints for the work of service.
- From self-focused "serve us" to service.
- From duplication of human services and ministries to partnering with existing services and ministries.
- From condemning the city to blessing the city and praying for it.
- From being a minister in a congregation to being a minister in a parish.[16]

These principles get our eyes off ourselves so we can focus on the needs of others. Perhaps addressing these issues will give you an opportunity to reflect on the demand to be taken care of because "I deserve better and more," which is so common in our culture today.

Charles Sykes wrote *A Nation of Victims: The Decay of the American Character*, describing how entitlement has become the norm in virtually every segment of our society, including our churches. Your church can be a beacon of hope and light in the darkness of self-absorbed victimhood. Certainly some people have been victimized, but they don't have to remain victims. The glorious message of the cross is that Jesus Christ redeems souls, fills hearts, forgives sins, heals hurts, and changes lives.

One of the greatest messages of the church today is that we may be wounded, but we can find genuine hope and healing in Jesus Christ. Part of our hope is that God has a

---

16 "Building the Externally Focused Church," Christian Washington, www.leadnet.org/resources/resources.asp

wonderful plan for our lives, a plan to use each of us in his incredible, eternal desire to bless all people. We can experience the measure of his great grace, because none of us deserve such a fantastic future.

It all boils down to this: God's great grace has changed your life and mine, and we deeply desire to see him touch the lives of others. As we become more aware of specific needs in our communities, and as we are gripped with a passion for God to use us to meet those needs, we will look for every available resource we can find. That's what partnerships are all about. We need to be wise in selecting the right organizations for the right events, and we need to connect the purpose of the event with a core purpose of in the church. But for God's sake, we need to be as strategic and creative as we can possibly be in order to be effective tools in his hands.

> *But for God's sake, we need to be as strategic and creative as we can possibly be in order to be effective tools in his hands.*

Reflection

1. What are three needs in your community? (Think about areas such as marriage, parenting, finances, food and shelter, purpose in life, crime, health, etc.)

What are some specific ways you can address those needs?

2. List the organizations (businesses, nonprofits, agencies, government, etc.) that are active in meeting those needs.

3. What are the media outlets in your area?

4. Who are people in your church who have connections with the organizations and media outlets you have listed?

5. Brainstorming: What are some events that might accomplish your goals to enhance outreach, develop leaders, and provide places for people to serve?

chapter 7

Strategy #3: Conduct Faith-Building Events

"That same day Jesus went out of the house and sat by the lake. Such large crowds gathered around him that he got into a boat and sat in it, while all the people stood on the shore. Then he told them many things in parables" (Matt 13:1-3).

Why Conduct Big Events?

The work of the Spirit of God is intensely personal. Each of us is invited individually to respond to the gospel. Our parents can't trust Christ for us, nor our spouses, our children, or our friends. Each of us comes alone, with empty hands and open hearts.

However, the message of the gospel is often communicated to large audiences. The gospel accounts tell us over and over again that Jesus spoke to "crowds" and "multitudes." He proclaimed his words of reconciliation and hope from hillsides, shorelines, and Temple plazas to anyone who would listen. Big events were an integral part of his ministry, and his example was passed along to his disciples.

On the first day of the church, crowds were present to witness the arrival of the Holy Spirit. Luke records that three thousand responded in faith to Peter's gospel message that day. Many others responded to the disciples' preaching in the days that followed—so many that the disciples were forced to reconfigure the leadership of the church to include deacons and elders. Years later, Paul's ministry was also characterized by large gatherings where he preached to crowds in synagogues and city plazas.

In the ongoing history of the church, we find hundreds of accounts of people who spoke to multitudes. Jonathan Edwards and George Whitefield, for example, preached to thousands in the open air and in churches during the Great Awakening in America.

Around the turn of the 20th century, another remarkable leader used large events to take the message of Christ to millions of unreached people. John Mott graduated from Cornell University, Phi Beta Kappa. Like many other young Christians of his day, he was gripped with a desire to address the needs of people who had never heard the name of Christ. For several decades, he served as the leader of the Student Volunteer Movement—one of the greatest missions movements in history as 30,000 of the best and brightest young men and women left behind fame and fortune for the oblivion of foreign missions.

During that time, John Mott often spoke to tens of thousands in India or China. His messages often lasted four hours or more, even though he spoke in the open air with no microphone. And quite often, his audience refused to let him close. Even after several hours, they would yell to ask him to preach more to them.

Mott's passion was Jesus Christ. He combined evangelism and leadership development into a seamless whole as he took young leaders with him everywhere he went, demonstrating zeal, wisdom, and strategy for expanding the kingdom of God. Mott's influence was so broad and profound that President Woodrow Wilson wanted to appoint him to be the United States Ambassador to China. Mott replied that he appreciated the honor, but declined because of "the priority of a greater calling."

In 1946, after years of leading one of the most amazing missions movements in history, Mott was awarded the Nobel Peace Prize for his impact on people around the world. In his final public appearance in 1954, Mott rose to speak at a large meeting. The audience was prepared for a lengthy message, but he said only, "Gentlemen, when John Mott is dead, remember him as an evangelist."

Mott wedded the dual goals of reaching the world with the gospel and training leaders. The young men and women he trained were exposed to his model of ministry. They witnessed firsthand the hard but strategic work of planning, organizing, orchestrating, and following up the fruit of big events. Mott's disciples followed his example, and millions were presented with the gospel who had never before heard the name of Jesus.

Some people may think that big events only feed big egos. Certainly we have reason to suspect the motives of certain people, such as the Pharisees in Jesus' day and numerous figures in our own time. But that's no reason to do away with big events altogether. When the compassion and goodness of God touch our own hearts, the fire of his love will purify our motives and we will increasingly want what he wants. Jesus and Paul didn't always wait until people came to them. Quite often, God's love compelled them speak to available crowds.

> *When the compassion and goodness of God touch our own hearts, the fire of his love will purify our motives and we will increasingly want what he wants.*

In our church and in countless other churches and mission agencies across the world, large events have a powerful impact. Some of the benefits include:

- reaching out to far more people with the transforming power of the gospel;

- imparting vision and building the faith of those involved;
- providing opportunities for existing leaders to sharpen their skills;
- involving many others by providing opportunities to serve Christ and people;
- building a team spirit among those who work together for the success of the event; and
- creating or expanding the positive reputation of the church as it meets needs in the community.

Those benefits are well worth the effort, but they are only realized if the leadership team plans and promotes the event wisely, leads with enthusiasm, clarity and grace, and generates the involvement and excitement of every person in the church.

Some church leaders have told me they are hesitant to risk planning and conducting faith-building events. Some are afraid of failure, some are already overwhelmed and can't imagine adding to their loads, and some struggle with pride and humility. Others may have seen leaders who called attention to themselves when a big plan succeeded, and they don't want to appear to be (or actually be) prideful. But we will all wrestle with our fallen natures and our impure motives until we see Christ face to face. While we are in this life, we can either withdraw because we realize our motives are suspect, or we can fight our natural tendencies for the glory of God.

Oswald Sanders told the story of a 19th-century itinerant Scottish minister who developed a consistent and effective means to give God glory instead of honoring himself. Sanders wrote, "When Robert Murray McCheyne experienced times of blessing in his ministry, on returning home from the service, he would kneel down and symbolically place the crown of success on the brow of the Lord to whom he knew it rightly belonged. This practice helped to save him from the peril of arrogating to himself the glory which belonged to God."[17]

This simple physical act was McCheyne's demonstration of thankfulness to God, and it reinforced the fact that God gave him the talents to use in people's lives. As we look at the important strategy of big events, we need to keep our motivations in perspective. These events are planned and conducted to honor Jesus Christ, to take his message of hope to as many people as possible, and to build leaders who are willing to take risks to expand the kingdom of God. As the Lord blesses our efforts, we can get off our horses and put the crown of victory on his head where it belongs.

Remember Your Church's Strengths

Every church has a personality. If the pastor has been there for a while, the church's personality usually reflects his own. Similarly, every church has a particular set of strengths, and those strengths almost always shape the direction and the nature of the church's big events.

Some churches are known for terrific teaching of the Scriptures, so their big events may be Bible conferences. Others are devoted to healing the hurts of the addicted, the victims of abuse, and the grieving. Those churches may conduct large recovery events. Still others may enjoy wonderful music or drama. Or perhaps the pastor and his staff are gifted in training other church leaders in ministry philosophy and strategy, like Willow Creek and Saddleback.

No matter what the particular personality of an individual church, though, we have a common purpose to reach the lost. Some of the big events a church sponsors each year

---

17 Sanders, *Spiritual Leadership,* p. 150.

should be devoted to that specific and crucial purpose. Teaching, recovery, and every other "personality" can adapt to outreach. For example, a church that is strong in teaching the Scriptures might sponsor John Piper for a series. The title of the series could be chosen to appeal to a wide range of people, and the entire community could be invited. The church would need to communicate clearly with the speaker (John Piper would love this approach!), and the series would touch lives far beyond the church newsletter list.

Our church is in an area where only five percent of the people attend church on a regular basis. The majority of our big events, therefore, focus on outreach. In response to God's leading, four times each year we concentrate our efforts to invite as many people as possible and put on the most attractive program for them. These four times are our July Fourth Celebration, the Harvest Festival, Christmas, and Easter. But any and every holiday is an opportunity to host a big event and reach out into the community.

Before my brother Gene helped me begin our church in Carson Valley, he coordinated big events for his church, which used Mother's Day as one of its outreaches. In fact, Barna believes that Mother's Day rivals Easter and Christmas as a day when families attend church together. If Mom wants her family to go to church on that day, they go. It provides a wonderful opportunity to show the community your church cares about their families.

I have already described our July Fourth Celebration and Harvest Festival in some detail, so let me address the two other major dates on our church calendar. We find that in every community, even those where so few regularly attend worship, people have a warm feeling for family and faith on Christmas and Easter. They may not even think of coming to church any other days of the year, but they have some sense that those two dates are important.

Our post-Christian culture has dulled people's sense of the actual meanings of these events, but it hasn't completely obliterated them yet. So we pull out all the stops for these services and encourage our members to invite their neighbors, family, and friends. They put first-class fliers in the hands of every person in the community, warmly greet each person who walks in our doors, present the very finest singing and drama, and follow up by contacting every person who attends. This effort takes a lot of planning, orchestration, and sweat, but it is well worth it.

This effort takes a lot of planning, orchestration, and sweat, but it is well worth it.

In addition, we conduct several other internal big events each year which focus on specific biblical themes. We previously joined Saddleback's "40 Days of Adventure" to teach people how to live a life of faith, and followed up by doing "30 Days of Easter" which teaches our people about the passion and sacrifice of Christ. The Easter series culminated, of course, on Easter Sunday when the place is packed with people from the community. In fact, we saw close to 250% of our average weekly attendance on Easter weekend.

We also use our baptism services as special events for our church body. We used to baptize people in someone's pool or hot tub with only a small group gathered, but we found that the testimonies of changed lives are so powerful that we wanted those services to become more central to the life of the church. Now we put a hot tub on the platform and conduct the baptism and testimonies during our services. I come from a tradition that treated baptism as important but somewhat routine. Baptisms are not routine at our church. They are parties! They celebrate the work of God's Spirit to transform lives. The excitement generated by these events is building a legacy which creates heightened anticipation for the next one, and the next, and on and on.

In most cases, it is wise for the church to host big events on site, but occasionally a neutral setting is more effective. A church in Austin, Texas, rented the ballroom at the Hyatt Hotel every Thursday night for six weeks to conduct a series on "Finding and Following Your Life's Purpose." They advertised in the newspaper and invited people from all over the community, targeting executives and professionals. It was a wonderful success. Each week the crowds grew, and the enthusiasm was infectious. The church saw a significant influx of people attending services as a direct result of their efforts to go where it was most convenient for people and address a relevant topic that rang their bells.

Our church leaders also support big events sponsored by other organizations, such as Women of Faith and Promise Keepers. We endorse concentrated applications of spiritual effort and energy that accomplish personal and community objectives. When we send people to these events, we pray that they will connect meaningfully to God and to others around them, and that God will work deeply in their lives to accomplish his gracious purposes.

These days pastors and church leaders don't have to re-create the wheel for every age group and every need. Good and godly organizations are dedicated to providing the finest environments and materials to assist the church by hosting faith-building events. We simply need to choose wisely and promote them well. Then, when these people return after God has touched their hearts, we can rejoice and enjoy the fruit that has been produced.

The church should not, however, abdicate its role in originating some of the big events that expand people's vision and meet their needs. Otherwise, the subtle message is that while church may be fine, members need to go elsewhere to experience new and fresh spiritual vitality. Before long, the reputation, role, and authority of the church are weakened.

Many of the existing internal events in churches are natural avenues for outreach. For example, one church conducted a class using James Dobson's series on "Raising Boys." Many parents in that church left other classes to attend this series because the subject was so vital to them. But the leaders of this church didn't see the opportunity to use the series for outreach. Thousands of other parents in that area care just as much as the church members about learning to raise their sons. The series was a big success for those who came, but it could have had a far bigger and broader impact if the community had been invited.

Almost every family in every community in the country is interested in topics like marriage, parenting, finances and handling debt, and finding purpose and meaning in life. Does the church have anything to say about these things? You bet it does! Can the church use its classes on these topics as outreach tools? Of course. Entrepreneurs can help the church understand how to position these events to reach the maximum number of people.

Does the church have anything to say about these things? You bet it does!

Andy Stanley, a pastor in the Atlanta area who has written about the need for creativity in ministry, has said the church needs to invest in relationships and invite people to events that will make a difference in their lives. Many of our churches are ingrown and fail to encourage people to have meaningful, authentic relationships with unbelievers. But when such relationships exist, we can use any and every event to invite them to activities that can meet their needs.

One role of church leaders is to provide events that are attractive and life-changing. Then people will invite their friends. Quite often, though, the first audience we need to impress with excellence is our own members. When they are sure they won't be embarrassed by a poor performance at the big event, they will bring their friends. For this reason, expect your first big event to be attended primarily by your own people. As their trust grows, they will bring a lot of people.

Using faith-building events to reach out to the community and build leaders can have positive results you never expect. For example, one church hosted a crafts fair. Artists from all over the area displayed their work, and many people in the community came to the church facility for the event. That in itself was a success. But as an added bonus, the church developed the reputation of being a place where creativity is valued, so artists and those who appreciate art began attending the church.

How do church leaders decide which faith-building events to host, and which to support by sending their people to attend? The answer is in the leaders' experience of God's heart as they listen intently to God's Spirit. As we watch and pray, God will enflame a desire to meet certain needs. Our desire for multitudes to respond to the gospel and for leaders to be built will shape our plans for big events. I'm convinced that people in every church have a heart to make a difference for Christ, yet many of them don't feel the freedom to dream, plan, and work. As leaders, it is our responsibility be good examples in dreaming and planning to touch thousands of lives. As we do, we teach the people in our churches to dream and plan as well.

As leaders, it is our responsibility be good examples in dreaming and planning to touch thousands of lives.

Some churches try to do too many big events. Their desire is in the right place, but they need to think more strategically. It is far better to have a few outstanding events than to have so many that excellence is compromised. At first, realize that you have limited resources, and focus your attention on two or three events that are the heart and soul of your message to the community. Pour your energies into these events. Use them to reach out to lost people, and use them to build solid leaders. As your resources of gifted people, funds, and space expand, ask God to guide you to another event, and conduct it with the same level of excellence. If you ask people in our area about Carson Valley Christian Center, they will tell you two things: It's a church that has big events that are a lot of fun, and they are people who care about the arts. Those traits are very attractive to people in this area.

Get the Word Out

At our church, we use practically every activity and every event as outreach, except for a couple which are designed specifically for fellowship. Once a year we have a big fellowship for our church family, and we focus our attention on sharing and caring for one another. We also have a special baptism at Lake Tahoe in the summer. That, too, is designed for our church family. Except for those two events, we build an outreach component into every activity. Our planning and praying for all the other events are devoted to reaching the unreached in our area.

By far, the most significant way to get the word out about an event is word of mouth from excited people. A smiling face and a cheerful invitation are far more effective than any other marketing tools, but God can use other media to supplement and reinforce direct, people-to-people invitations.

I've mentioned that 80 percent of homes in our area get a local newspaper, and we use inserts in the paper to promote many of our events. When I lived in Southern California, I would never have used that strategy because most people don't seem to read inserts in the local newspapers. In the same way, the local cable channel is a very useful promotional tool in this area, but it wouldn't be as effective in other parts of the country.

Tailor your promotional strategies according to the culture and resources of your specific community. Just remember that you can spend $10,000 on media promotion, but if your people aren't excited about the event, your money will be wasted. Your first priority is to impart a vision for the event to your people. Then your print and other promotions will have far more impact.

Many pastors don't have a background in advertising, but some people in their congregations probably do. My friend, Andy Vom Steeg, is the pastor of New Vintage Church (formerly First Baptist Church) in Santa Rosa, California. Andy looked for people who could help him design and develop a promotional strategy for their events. By making just a few inquiries, he soon had five people with marketing backgrounds who became the promotional team for that church. Those people probably wondered if God would ever use the skills they had developed. It only took their pastor a short time to find them, challenge them, and get them involved before their considerable expertise was being directed by their desire to please God and make a difference in people's lives. The same abilities used to sell cars, hamburgers, houses, or widgets are now being used to expand the kingdom of God.

Most churches in America contain at least one person with marketing skills. As church leaders, we need to find those people, give them encouragement and direction, and let them go to work with creativity and joy. We have a lot to learn from such people as they use their gifts and experiences to serve Christ, the church, and the community. To get started, you might invite a marketing expert in your church to a staff or lay leadership meeting and ask that person to give input on how to touch the lives of people in the community. The interaction will be informative and instructive for all of you.

Promotion should be designed to communicate the value of the event and the benefits to those who attend. It is a cardinal rule (for those with integrity, anyway) to "under-promise and over-deliver." In the movie "Top Gun," Tom Cruise was told, "Don't write checks you can't cash." The same principle applies in every area of life. The church needs to avoid making promises it can't keep.

If you promise to provide "quality childcare" but a mother finds her toddler unattended with soiled underwear, you will have lost the privilege of communicating the grace of God to that person. If you tell the public that your music is upbeat and contemporary but you actually have old hymns accompanied by an organ, the people who came for the music won't come back—and they'll tell their friends not to go there, either. Truth in advertising requires us to go to work long before the actual event to be sure we can provide what we promise. Only when the planning and first stages of implementation are complete can we be assured that we can deliver what we hope to provide.

For instance, our promotional material for our Fourth of July Celebration (print, radio, and cable television) tells people they will enjoy game booths and activities, great music, food, and rides—and it will all be free. We deliver on every one of those promises, and people genuinely appreciate it. Each of those things requires a lot of planning and work, but the result is a lot of happy people, wonderful conversations, and outstanding pre-evangelism. The credibility of our church has risen with every event because we have a rigorous commitment to deliver what we promise.

All of our promotional efforts encourage people to respond in some way. Each brochure, insert, radio spot, or cable ad includes an invitation. We want people to take some kind of action, but we tailor the actual response to the event. Often we hand out tickets to people in our church and ask them to give a ticket to everyone they invite. Sometimes we ask people to call our church office to reserve a place, especially if we are providing meals. When we use tickets, we have people at the door with buckets to collect them. Of course, we welcome people without tickets, too. But a ticket is a tool that reminds people they have been invited and have made a commitment to come. We typically don't use any kind of response device (such as a ticket or a confirmation call) at our broadest outreach events. But we do use them when we focus on a specific group of people and want to meet a particular need in their lives.

In promoting your church's big events, look for a "hook" that compels people to come. For the Fourth of July Celebration, we try to offer something interesting for every age group, and we describe those things in our promotional material. For Easter, we promote many things, including an egg hunt for the little kids. Many children in our neighborhoods find out about the hunt and get excited about it. And many parents come to the Easter Celebration primarily because their little children are excited about finding the eggs.

The hook is what compels people to come, and it gives them a pleasant sense of expectation. It is the promise of fun, meaning, food, connections with people, spiritual insight, or anything else you offer at your events. When we "under-promise and over-deliver," we exceed the expectations of people and we become heroes in their eyes—especially to parents when our activities meet their children's needs.

Let Big Events Shape Leaders

Wonderful things can happen when an event is conducted with excellence by people who serve gladly, but be sure to be realistic about the costs in time, money, and effort. Faith-building events have a big impact, but they also require the leader's time and significant resources from those who are involved. Be sure to plan early, to ask plenty of questions, and to form a team of people who are both skilled and motivated.

The selection of the team is perhaps the most important task of a leader. If he selects wisely, the team will encourage each other, blend their skills, and produce a life-changing event. If he selects the wrong people or fails to impart adequate vision for the event, the result may be conflict, lethargy, and a poor event. Previous failures to select wisely could be a primary reason why more leaders are hesitant to plan big events today.

A big event will be either a drain or a stimulus to its organizers, and the pastor needs to be sensitive to each person's attitude following the event. The perspective of the pastor and other top church leaders usually influences the motivation of each person involved. Some people perceive such activities as a hindrance that gets in the way of what they are called to do. If so, they may use guilt to get people to do the work they don't want to do themselves. Or more commonly, they simply won't plan for the event in the first place.

On the other hand, if the top leaders see these events as wonderful gifts from God to accomplish the dual purposes of touching the community and building faith and skills in rising leaders, organizers will relish and cherish these opportunities to serve together. The events become a channel for them to use their abilities for God's glory and a platform to communicate the love of God to people in their communities.

At that time, I can look back and think, "I'm really tired, but God did some incredible things in us and through us." There's no other feeling quite like that.

When a group of people works hard to pull off a Fourth of July Celebration, a Harvest Festival, or a 40 Day Adventure of Faith, those people are forced to communicate, to understand one another, to find common ground when they disagree, and to learn the value of teamwork. One of my favorite moments is late at night after 50 of us have worked like dogs to produce an excellent event. At that time, I can look back and think, "I'm really tired, but God did some incredible things in us and through us." There's no other feeling quite like that.

Additional goals of these big events are to sharpen the leadership skills of those who oversee teams, to identify rising leaders, and to encourage each person to serve the Lord gladly. Those goals aren't achieved without intentional effort. Key leaders have to think, plan, and pray about each person's role, and must find the balance between challenging others with a difficult task and letting them find a comfortable place where they can serve fairly easily. To find that balance, we have to be aware of how each person is motivated, responds to challenges, and tolerates change. It's the job of the key leader—and a delight when it is done correctly—to know people and tailor their roles so they are encouraged and challenged.

Some people already have the habit of serving others, but big events offer a wide array of service opportunities, so that even those new to the church can be involved. When people first see that God has used them to touch another life, the experience may catapult them to a new level of spiritual receptivity and excitement. You can see the joy of serving in people's eyes—sometimes in people who never thought the Lord could use them.

Involving a large group of people in service is a way of building community within the church. Serving together creates deeper bonds. The shared experience may form a connection that produces genuine friendship, and the body is strengthened.

Build a Team

Bookstores are full of books on leadership and team-building, so we don't need to write another book at this point. However, I want to identify five phases of developing a great team to organize and lead faith-building events.

Phase 1: Identify the scope of the event.

The broad planning phase is usually conducted with the top leaders of the church and identifies the purpose, intended audience, topic, facilities, promotion, and timing of the event. This phase also includes some rough budgeting of finances and other resources.

Phase 2: Identify the team leaders.

As the plan takes more definite shape, the roles and responsibilities are clarified. At this point, you will identify the men and women who will be asked to take the top leadership positions for the event. Each of these people will oversee a team, so the designated leaders must be able to recruit, train, encourage, and direct others.

I recommend you ask God to give you a person who will be your coordinator of big events for your church. This person will have a passion for these events because he or she understands the incredible benefits that can come from them. In addition, this person must have organizational skills

I recommend you ask God to give you a person who will be your coordinator of big events for your church.

and good relationships with the staff. This role is at times demanding and consuming, but the pressure is cyclical, not continual. The coordinator's faith, vision, and skills can make a tremendous difference in the growth of the church. Over time, he or she will create a climate of excellence so that the church is known in the community as "that group of people who provide great events and have a blast doing it."

Phase 3: Recruit key people.

I'm convinced many members in our churches are underemployed in God's kingdom. Numerous skilled and motivated people would love to have significant roles, but we aren't asking them to get involved. They may be trained in administration, marketing, counseling, arts, or hundreds of other areas. Discover what type of service motivates them by tapping into their skills and hearts' desires. Go beyond the superficial level, and find out what makes them tick. Go places with them. Notice what bores them, what excites them, and what makes them cry. One of my roles as a leader is to network people with similar passions so they encourage each other. All this takes time, but it is well worth it.

Don't take many risks with the selection of key roles. Ask God for wisdom and direction, and look for people who will be "champions with a grand-opening attitude." They should be people who are committed to excellence, enthusiastic, and who have a proven track record for building an effective team. This is a crucial moment in the life of the event. In this phase you will meet face to face with those you have selected to impart your vision, describe the specific roles, and listen carefully to their ideas.

Phase 4: Visualize the event.

Help your team leaders anticipate as many opportunities and obstacles as you can. This exercise will enable them to capitalize on the successes and avoid potential problems. Think about each aspect of the event: music, the speaker, entertainment, greeters, sign-ups, signage, parking, bad weather contingencies, food, etc. For example, one of the most common mistakes in planning events where meals are served is failure to realize that 500 people don't move quickly through a single serving line. When people have to wait too long, they get impatient. Use multiple lines, stagger the serving times, and/or make sure your cooks or food service people are prepared early.

Good planning and good anticipation of potential problems will minimize confusion or wasted time at your event. Being prepared enables the team leaders to focus on the team and encourage them instead of running around in a panic trying to solve unforeseen problems.

Phase 5: Be flexible.

Pastor Chuck Smith of Calvary Chapel has said, "Blessed are the flexible, for they shall not be broken." His leadership "beatitude" applies very well to big events. One of the most attractive traits of a good and godly leader is one who plans and prepares well, but who trusts in the goodness and the sovereignty of God. No matter how well you have planned, things can go wrong. The sound system chooses that moment to quit, the speaker's plane is late, the caterer spills a platter of food, your child gets sick, and on and on and on. Those things happen. The question is, "How will you respond?"

All of us have been on the receiving end of leaders who have failed to plan and then blamed others when an event was unsuccessful, and many of us have watched as an obsessive-compulsive control freak tried to dominate every person and every detail of an event. That takes all the joy out of serving on a team. Good planning, joy in serving, and trust in God combine to make an excellent leader, one who produces a quality event and who also builds strength and joy into the lives of other team members. (A planning worksheet is found at the end of this chapter.)

I know if I've done a good job of planning, selecting team leaders, and equipping them to do their jobs if my role becomes "management by walking around." My role then becomes "chief encourager," and I tell people how much I appreciate what they are doing. I do a little trouble-shooting if they need help, and I get to watch them serve God while he uses them to touch the hearts of others. If they need some water, I go get them a bottle. If they need a break, I'll step in for a while. Instead of being the top dog in the church, I become their servant. That's my kind of job!

No matter how well you plan, strange things can happen. One of my lasting memories is of an event that occurred when we were trying to build up our team before the launch of our church. About 50 of us were meeting on Sundays for worship in the ballroom of a casino in Carson City. My goal was to showcase the quality and excellence we wanted to produce when our church was launched about five months later.

I thought we had several microphones with long cords to use with the boom box cassette and CD system, but we only had one microphone—and it had a short cord. In fact, the cord was so short that Roy Conover, our song leader at the time, had to lean over the boom box to sing! What a sight! What a message to our leaders! And you can be sure, those 50 people remembered that day. On our fifth anniversary, we created a small "sculpture" to commemorate the occasion. To this day, Roy (who is now on staff as Congregational Care Pastor) is known as "the guy who had to lean over the boom box"!

Evaluating Big Events

Some of us are so burned out after a big event that we collapse in exhaustion. Be sure to save some time and energy after an event so you and your team leaders can reflect on the wonderful things God did at the event and the things you could have done a bit better. In your evaluation, you will focus on:

- the planning process, purpose, and audience;
- the timing and budget;
- the selection of team leaders and team members;
- each aspect of the program;
- facilities;
- promotion; and
- follow-up strategy.

In our church, we want our events to be fun—not only for newcomers, but for our team leaders and team members, too. We want those who serve to see God using them to make a difference in other's lives. If these goals are not met for those who serve, the goals of the event probably won't be accomplished, either.

Many pastors might read this chapter and say, "I'd like to have faith-building events like that, but I'm already overwhelmed." I would respond, "Yes, I know you are. I've been there myself. These events, though, are invaluable in accomplishing God's purposes for your church, so what else are you going to stop so you can devote your energies to these events?"

Continuing to do the same things in the same ways just won't accomplish the purposes of changing lives, reaching the

In our church, we want our events to be fun—not only for newcomers, but for our team leaders and team members, too. We want those who serve to see God using them to make a difference in other's lives.

community with the gospel, and building dynamic leaders who serve with passion and joy.

Rick Warren has said that one mistake church leaders make—especially those who plant churches—is to try to build the church from the inside out. They focus their efforts on the few who are already faithful and tend to neglect the masses.

The pattern in the life of Christ, however, is to build from the outside in. He never neglected his public, large-group ministry. Over and over again, the Savior fed, healed, and spoke to crowds. They rarely understood what his mission was. They came for some bread and fish, or for physical healing, or to be entertained by his strange sayings—but they came. Jesus certainly didn't insist on perfect motivations from those who were interested enough to come to hear him. Nor did he always speak to them in general, positive terms. Sometimes he spoke hard words to the multitude, just as he did to his disciples. And in some cases, "many of his disciples turned back and no longer followed him" (John 6:66).

Sometimes I stand in front of a crowd at our church and speak hard words of abject commitment to Jesus Christ. I know some of those people probably won't return in the next few weeks, but I am determined to emulate the ministry of Christ. We are committed to gathering the multitudes in large meetings, but we are also committed to speaking the clear and compelling words of Christ to them.

A corollary to this commitment is that we welcome anybody and everybody to come to hear the life-changing word of Christ. The leaders of some churches have lived in their "holy huddles" so long that they have lost sight of Christ's invitation for those from the highways and byways to come to him. Those stodgy, ingrown Christians only feel comfortable with worshipers who repent quickly, clean up their lives, and wash their bodies so they are nicer and cleaner.

A number of bikers come to our church, and some of our female attendees have been (and may still be) prostitutes. Whenever I see a rough-looking person walk in our door, I make a point of going to him or her, shaking hands, and welcoming the person warmly. I want those men and women (and those in our church) to know that we, like Jesus, love those who are lost, who are hurting, and who may have been cast aside by society.

> *Whenever I see a rough-looking person walk in our door, I make a point of going to him or her, shaking hands, and welcoming the person warmly.*

A few local law enforcement officers have told me, "At first, it was hard for me to attend your church." I asked them why, and they responded, "Because when I looked around, I saw people we'd busted days, weeks, or months ago. But then I realized this is the best place in the world for them to be. If they're here, there's something good going on in their lives. Thanks for your ministry to them." I consider these words to be a wonderful compliment to our church.

I enjoy the academic tools I gained from college, seminary, and doctoral studies. Those studies are all stimulating to me, but nothing revs my engines like seeing a life changed. That's what keeps me up at night and is the reason I wake up with hope and joy in the morning.

Faith-building events require leaders who are willing to plan well, work hard, and risk failure. In the parable of the talents, the servants willing to take those risks were honored. Paul said he "pressed on toward the goal for the prize of the upward call of God in Christ Jesus." He took regular risks to fulfill his calling to reach people for his Savior. And don't forget those Yukon miners. They had a vision of great riches, so they were willing to take enormous risks and suffer severe hardships to achieve their goals. We can learn from all of these examples to start with a vision of a great treasure. That vision gives us hope, tenacity, and courage as we plan well, work hard, and take the necessary risks to reach the lost for the sake of Christ.

Reflection

1. Describe one or two of the most successful and encouraging outreach events you've ever seen.

2. What is your church's personality? How can you construct events consistent with this personality that will also serve as outreaches to the community?

3. What are the most effective avenues of promotion in your community? Which of these are you using?

4. Who are some people in your church with expertise in marketing?

5. In what ways can you envision big events as tools to develop leaders in your church?

6. Take some time to pray and think about how God may want to take your church to a new level in using faith-building events to touch your community and build your leaders. Write your thoughts and germinal plans here.

Event Checklist
Tailor this checklist to meet the needs of each specific event.

Scheduling
— Select the site and facilities

— Determine the target audience

— Pick the event coordinator

— Select and confirm program content (speakers, music, emcee, etc.), theme, dates, fees, travel, accommodations

— Select the date: research potential conflicts in the church and the city

— Identify potential partnerships

— Determine the promotion plan

— Projected attendance / Cost-revenue analysis

— Budget

Brochure, Inserts, Fliers
— Dates

— Theme

— Speakers' bios and pics or description of activities

— Pertinent info: map, directions, benefits, audience, schedule, etc.

— Quantity needing to be printed: for the church, mailings, booths, etc.

Promotion

— Brochure mailings: Quantity to each contact, drop dates

— Booths

— Articles in the newspaper

— Promo at the church

— PSA's on radio, TV

— Special promotions

— Master Plan: schedule for all promotions

Pre-Event Preparations

— Select and confirm the emcee

— Prepare a detailed schedule for the emcee and sound/projection people, including nuances of the setup, bios, things to know, etc.

— Obtain any materials needed

— Format seminar handouts (if needed)

— Plan and organize the registration table, greeters, etc.

— Have evaluation form written and printed

— Arrange facilities: room, signage, registration table, AV equipment

— Arrange refreshments

— Keep up with registrations (if needed) through the church office

— Nametags

— Determine taping requirements, if any

— Set up booktable: Consider presentation, inventory control, pricing, discounts, types of payment available, etc.

— Check sound system, other AV needs

Booktable

— Determine who will be in charge of the booktable during the event

— Determine the titles and quantities of each title

— Order the books, using shipping instructions to the church (Get the name of a responsible person on staff who will take care of the books)

— Plan your announcements about book sales

— Tape order form (if applicable)

Registration at the event (if needed)

— Dry run of the process the week before the event

— Signs

— Payment information and processes

— Information on computer or on registration forms (or both)

— Nametags

— Prepare manuals for pickup

— Adequate staffing of the registration table to ensure quick processing

— Anticipate bad weather needs (Umbrella escorts? Covered drop off?)

Program

— Gracious ushers to welcome people

— Warm, competent emcee

— Mike and sound system working smoothly

— Begin and end each session on time: time cards

— Anticipate needs of attenders: restroom breaks, Q & A, etc.

— Refreshments on time, appropriate temperature, etc.

— Prayer, dependence, God-centered atmosphere

— At the end, pass out evaluations: give time to complete and collect

— Gracious ending

— Point people to the next event: content, dates, etc.

Post-Event

— Clean up, pack up bookstore and room

— Get speaker to the airport on time

— Do a post-seminar evaluation with the emcee and team leaders

— Coordinate any orders for materials if the booktable ran out

— Compile evaluations

— Accounting

— Make a list of things to do and things to avoid next time

— Update mailing list

— Thank-you notes to appropriate people (leadership team, partners, etc.)

— Follow-up letter to those who attended (if needed)

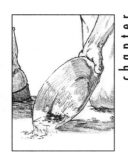

chapter 8

Strategy #4: Everyone's a 10—Get 'Em Moving!

"But to each one of us grace has been given as Christ apportioned it. . . . From him the whole body, joined and held together by every supporting ligament, grows and builds itself up in love, as each part does its work" (Eph 4:7,16).

Pastor Wayne Cordeiro of Hope Chapel in Oahu, Hawaii, has said, "Everyone is a 10 somewhere. The task of a leader is to help people identify where they are a 10."

Not everyone is known for high I.Q. levels or artistic skill, but every person has a place where he or she has the highest capacity for effective service in God's kingdom. In real estate, property is evaluated on its "best use." Wayne Cordeiro was talking about each *person's* best use in serving Christ. Entrepreneurs know they are a "10" in their skills and passions.

For instance, my "10" is in leading and speaking. I love to be involved in those activities, and God seems to bless my efforts there more than anything else I do. Sometimes people have come to me for counseling and later told me they were helped by my insights and encouragement. But when they walked out the door after the session, I felt exhausted, not energized. And when it comes to counseling, after two or three sessions with someone my usual advice is, "OK, you know what the problem is, so do the right thing and quit doing the wrong thing. Thanks for coming. God bless you."

At that point, they need to find someone more skilled in counseling than I am. So while some people may consider me a good counselor, I would never say counseling is a "10" for me.

80/20

Churches use numerous tools and materials to help people discover their spiritual gifts, many of which can be very helpful. Above and beyond all those resources, though, is the question, "What are the things you do for the Lord that rev your engines, give you energy, and tap into your passions to please God?"

> *"What are the things you do for the Lord that rev your engines, give you energy, and tap into your passions to please God?"*

The "80/20 rule" applies in several areas of church life. We often hear that 20 percent of the people do 80 percent of the work, and we know that 20 percent of the activities in a church (or any organization) produce 80 percent of the results. Here, we could use the principle to suggest that the top 20 percent of a person's abilities and gifts accomplish 80 percent of God's design for him or her. We need to capitalize on that 20 percent as much as possible in our life, work, and service.

A primary task of church leadership is to help people identify God's divine design for them, the roles of service that bring light to their eyes and enflame their passions. When I suggest an area of involvement to a particular person and his eyes glaze over, he looks at his watch, or he changes the subject, I know I haven't suggested something that's in his top 20 percent of gifts and abilities.

The wonderful truth is that God has given each believer abilities to use as we serve him. He has made us remarkably complex creatures, and he calls us to participate in his incredible redemptive purposes. Leaders need to help people first identify their abilities and then use them effectively to complement each other so that the synergistic impact turns the world upside down. Paul wrote, "But to each one of us grace has been given as Christ apportioned it. . . . From him the whole body, joined and held together by every supporting ligament, grows and builds itself up in love, as each part does its work" (Eph 4:7,16). Effective leaders give people permission and encouragement to find their part and do it!

In our church, we encourage people to dream, to pray, and to ask God to lead them to be involved in existing ministries or start new ones. The one caveat is that people work together in teams. No one serves alone.

Two ladies in our church have begun a quilting ministry—something I never would have thought of myself. One lady is in her 70s and the other is in her 40s. They are passionate about their work, not because of the threads and patterns, but because of the impact it has on people in our community. The older lady makes quilts to show God's love to children who have been abused. The younger woman uses quilts to reach out to young mothers who often feel alone at home with small children. Both have developed partnerships with agencies in our area who identify abused children and young mothers, then these ladies present the girls and moms with beautiful quilts along with a message of love from Christ and from our church. These dear ladies are passionate about meeting needs, and God has led them to use their talents and skills in a unique way to show his love to others. That's exciting!

It Begins at the Top

John Wesley said, "Catch on fire with enthusiasm and people will come from miles to watch you burn." Passionate and effective service in the pews (or chairs, in our case) begins with passionate and effective service by the pastor and other leaders of our church. Passion and purpose attract others and instill them with hopes and dreams. The alternative is to allow adherence to empty bureaucracy deflate the dreams of the faithful.

Dreams are the stuff of leadership. Without them, we are only organizers at best.

Church members won't have dreams unless you do. They won't spread the joy of trusting God to do mighty things unless it first spreads from you to them. We must dream big even when we are tired and our zeal has dried up and blown away. We must dream big as we seek God's face and trust him to guide us in the adventure of seeing lives changed. Dreams are the stuff of leadership. Without them, we are only organizers at best.

One of the most powerful ways to enflame the hearts of people in our church is for me to share how God is fulfilling the dreams of people who are serving him. I carefully choose who will be the "heroes" in our church, and I am sure to give glory to the Lord, who is the author of the dream and the power behind the changed lives. Yet the flesh-and-blood examples in our midst are powerful motivators who challenge others to serve with enthusiasm, boldness, and gladness.

For a couple of years, my brother Gene was in charge of the refreshments and food at our services, but about three years ago, Debbie Logan kicked him out of the kitchen and began coordinating all our food services. Gene was happy to step aside because Debbie had a vision, and God gave her a plan. She asked several couples to form four teams, and those teams now provide light meals to about 500 people before our Saturday night services.

The people Debbie recruited love to cook, and they use their abilities to provide delicious meals. They are passionate about using their gift of hospitality. The Naus are from New England and serve during the winter, preparing delicious soups from authentic recipes from that region of the country. The Langdons are terrific bakers, so they fix wonderful breads and desserts. Other teams are known for other types of dishes.

Debbie's service and her ability to organize these teams have provided a wonderful environment for the ministry of the gospel at our church. People love to come! (I suspect some come just for the food, but that's fine with me. And my brother is glad to let others do the cooking.)

You may be a pastor who feels frustrated that few in your church have a dream of their own, or you may be an associate or other leader who is frustrated because your pastor doesn't seem to have a dream. It is not a leader's responsibility to give someone a dream. But regardless of our titles or roles, it is the responsibility of each of us to pursue God, to listen intently to his voice and tap into his heart, and to live our dream so joyfully and hopefully that others around us naturally want to follow our example. The senior pastor needs to live his dream, but so do the teacher of fourth grade boys and the coordinator of refreshments for the 9:30 service.

Perhaps you will find many around you with the same passions and the same sense of purpose; perhaps not. Your responsibility is to faithfully and enthusiastically pursue the Lord and his calling—and pray for more laborers with the same heart. If you are an entrepreneur, perhaps part of your calling is to galvanize others with the same heart for kingdom impact!

In Acts 6, Luke describes a situation when so many people were joining the church that the original disciples were overwhelmed with administration. Their solution was to select seven people to serve so they could focus their energies on prayer and preaching God's word. You will notice, though, that those who were selected were not just warm bodies who were assigned jobs. No, they were people who were passionate about Christ and his kingdom, who were "known to be full of the Spirit and wisdom." Stephen, in fact, was a zealous evangelist who became the church's first martyr.

In the same way, the purpose of our selection and delegation is not just to get people to do what we don't want to do. Our role is to look for people who have a dream or who make another's dream their own, people who love God and whose service provides them an avenue to use their skills to honor the Lord.

Characteristics of the Real Disease

I have learned a lot from Rick Warren's ministry at Saddleback Community Church. Rick describes his "target" in concentric circles, with the center being his top leadership. These circles move toward the center from the outer ring of the *community,* to the *crowd* that comes to events, to the *congregation* that worships at the church, to the *committed* who support every activity, and finally to the *core* of leadership.

At our church, leadership is not about titles or positions. Leaders have a servant's heart, and they meet others' needs in Jesus' name. Some churches depend on the pastor to be the source of every vision, every activity, and every decision. That's not the way we work, and it's not the model I see in the New Testament. My role as the pastor is to provide overall direction and vision. In addition, it is also my responsibility to stimulate each person to pursue God with all his heart, soul, mind, and strength so each one has his or her own God-given vision. We want to build a broad base of leaders with that kind of vision, so that far more people are looking to the Lord for direction and far more people are serving with passion and joy.

"Everyone is a 10" is a full-employment policy in the kingdom of God. We don't want to leave anybody out. As each part does its work, the whole body grows.

Athletes and entertainers structure their lives for peak performance, but the body of Christ often functions in a very different way. Athletes eat right, exercise religiously, and tone their bodies so they are at their optimum efficiency on the day of the event. In the same way, entertainers practice for hours and prepare with others in the band, symphony, or group so they are at their best when the lights come on and the crowd cheers.

Yet far too often, instead of preparing people for peak performance, the church uses them to fill positions in the organizational chart. We need a second grade teacher for Sunday school, and we find somebody —anybody!— who will say "Yes" to us.

My role as the pastor is to provide overall direction and vision. In addition, it is also my responsibility to stimulate each person to pursue God with all his heart, soul, mind, and strength so each one has his or her own God-given vision.

When Mary Ellen Hamilton was 18 years old, she was walking down the hall at church. A desperate Sunday school superintendent saw her. He stopped her and pleaded, "We don't have a teacher for the toddlers. You've got to help us out for a couple of weeks." Many years later when I was pastor of that church, Mary Ellen told me, "I've taught this class for 23 years, and Pastor, I need a break." Until that day, I had no idea how she had been placed in that role. She had been stuck there for 23 years!

Many churches operate much the same way. We have desperate needs, and we try to fill them with good-hearted, willing people before thinking whether or not the job fits the person's calling and passion. We keep them there as long as they are willing to serve, and in fact, we gauge their spiritual maturity by how long they are willing to serve without complaining.

We need a different value system. We need to help people find the place where they can fulfill their calling, serve in their area of giftedness, and see God use them in their sweet spot. We need to inspire people to excellence instead of using them to fill empty slots.

Before I left my position as a denominational executive in 1997 to start our new church, I met with 25 cutting-edge, entrepreneurial pastors of our denomination. We called this gathering "Churches of the Future" and discussed the essentials of leadership development and the characteristics of leaders who are infectious in their enthusiasm and commitment to fulfilling God's calling. These are the characteristics we considered:

Leaders are learners.

We live in the Information Age. People have far more knowledge at their fingertips than any time in history. Many of the people in our pews spend hours each day, and certainly each week, looking at research and reading the latest articles and books on topics that affect spiritual life. If we are going to be good leaders of these people who are learning so much so fast, we need to be constantly gleaning and interpreting new information.

An important part of continuous improvement is to arrange our schedules around our leadership gifts. Paul warned Timothy, "Do not neglect your gift" (I Tim 4:14). We need to continually hone the cutting edge of our lives and ministries so we can remain as effective as possible. One day, each of us will stand before Christ to give an account. On that day, we will tell him what we did to sharpen and use the abilities he gave us. If we "skate" along and use our raw abilities without sharpening them, we will have some success, but not as much as we would if we fine-tuned our insights and developed our skills.

All of us should be learners, but not all of us learn the same way. One of the tragedies of modern academics in the community and in the church is that we use the lecture format far too often. That method works well for auditory learners, but not for all. Broaden your teaching methods to facilitate auditory, tactile, and many other learning styles.

Leaders are visionaries.

True vision is not "pie in the sky" blind optimism. It is the creative connection between the present and the future, what is and what might be. George Barna defined vision as "a clear mental image of a preferable future, imparted by God to his chosen servants, based upon an accurate understanding of God, self, and circumstances."[18]

A vision that comes from God is both challenging and reasonable. It has the qualities of wisdom (James 3:13-18), but it stirs the heart to trust God for more—sometimes far more than we've ever seen before.

As I mentioned earlier, very few visionaries get their dreams directly from God. Most of us are "learned visionaries" whose hearts are stirred when we listen to another person share his dream of changing the present into a better future. We need to go to conferences where we are exposed to these kinds of people, and we

> *A vision that comes from God is both challenging and reasonable. It has the qualities of wisdom (James 3:13-18), but it stirs the heart to trust God for more—sometimes far more than we've ever seen before.*

18 George Barna, *Without a Vision the People Perish,* (Barna Research Group, 1991).

need to make trips to watch someone's vision unfold with our own eyes.

Some of us see an inherent conflict between vision and management. Ken Blanchard stated, "There are two parts to leadership . . . one is vision-casting and the other is implementation. You have to implement things that match your vision. And remember, the thinking that got you to where you are today will not get you where you need to go."[19]

Some of us have witnessed a wild-eyed visionary who failed to make much of a connection due to poor implementation, which resulted in many people being disappointed and hurt. On the other hand, we can focus on micromanagement to the point of avoiding all risks to remain safe and stable. Indeed, vision is infused with the desire for change, and change requires boldness and courage. Robert Kennedy once said, "Moral courage is a rarer commodity than bravery in battle or great intelligence. Yet it is the one essential, vital quality of those who seek to change a world that yields most painfully to change."

Leadership involves risk.

Vision and risk go hand in hand. Risk is the uncertainty of the future and the discontinuity of the present in the process of change. As I have watched pastors and church leaders for many years, I have noticed they tend to gravitate to two ends of the continuum. A few are cavalier about the unsettling impact change can have. Their attitude is, "We're making changes. Either get on the boat or get off. Either way is fine with me." Far more church leaders are on the other end. They are cautious and unwilling to cause any difficulties, incur any conflict, or upset anybody.

---

19 Ken Blanchard, quoted in NetFax.

When I was a young pastor, I was afraid to be too aggressive. My reticence restricted my leadership and blocked opportunities for others to trust God for more. Looking back, I can see that if I had been bolder in my vision, many people in that congregation would have displayed more faith, served with more enthusiasm, and had a greater impact.

By their very nature, organizations and institutions resist change. Everything moves to equilibrium and inertia. Even the most reasonable and obviously beneficial change is viewed as a threat. But wise leaders create a culture in which challenging the status quo is not only tolerated; it is embraced because people are first committed to the mission. Change is not valued simply because it is novel and breaks up boredom. It is a path to accomplish the mission. We then welcome questions and debate as a normal part of decision-making.

In a rich and honest environment, the leader and the group can pursue the middle ground between being cavalier and cautious. Growing churches—and growing people—are those who respond with both courage and wisdom to a God-given mission. They are brave enough to launch out into new waters, but smart enough to take along paddles, provisions, and people.

Machiavelli acknowledged the reality of fear as people face change, but he noted that many come around as they actually see and experience the benefits of change. He wrote, "There is nothing more difficult to carry out, nor more doubtful of success, nor more dangerous to handle, than to initiate a new order of things. For the reformer has enemies . . . who profit by the old order, and only luke-warm defenders . . . who profit by the new order. This luke-warmness arises partly from fear of their adversaries, who have law in their favor; and partly from the incredulity of mankind, who do not truly believe in anything new until they have actual experience of it."[20]

Some of us may think that we need to conquer our fear before we can proceed, but that's simply not true. Any honest soldier will tell you that he is afraid as he goes into the dangers of combat. Courage is taking action in spite of our fear, not in the absence of it. I am encouraged by the honesty of King David. He was one of the greatest leaders in history, yet his psalms show his bravery was often in the face of doubts, confusion, and fear. He poured out his heart to the Lord when he was being attacked and falsely accused:

"Be merciful to me, O God, for men hotly pursue me;
    all day long they press their attack.
My slanderers pursue me all day long;
    many are attacking me in their pride.
When I am afraid,
    I will trust in you" (Ps 56:1-3).

Many of us, especially men, never want to admit we are afraid of anything because we hate to show any weakness! I've talked to people who hadn't slept well for months because they were so worried about something, but when asked, they stated emphatically, "Everything's fine. No problem." I've talked to others who had lived with a knot in their stomachs for weeks. Same response, "Oh, it's just indigestion. I'm fine."

I've learned that when I become aware of my fears (of failure, of criticism, of not being valued, or whatever it may be), my awareness is a point of repentance. At that moment, I have a choice to continue in my fear, or like David, to focus on God's sovereignty and love. And I've learned that

---

20 Niccolo Machiavelli, *The Prince*, (Bantam Classic edition, originally published in 1513.)

the far better choice is to trust God with my present worries and my future.

Leadership produces change in other leaders.

People are accustomed to feeling used. At work, at school, and often at home, many of us feel like cogs in a giant machine. So when we are treated with respect, and especially when somebody truly wants us to experience the love of God, it is a breath of fresh air.

Jesus wanted his followers to experience all the Father had for them. He was direct in explaining that "the way of the cross" would at times be difficult and painful, yet any suffering would surely be offset by the sheer joy of seeing lives changed. The disciples left nets, tax collection boxes, and other comfortable vocations to follow an itinerant preacher. Why? Because he offered them something they had never dreamed of: authentic love and the adventure of their lives.

Because he offered them something they had never dreamed of: authentic love and the adventure of their lives.

We have been given an incredible privilege of providing leadership over the flocks of God. Let them see authentic love and watch them follow us on a great adventure of their own.

Love and adventure sound great, don't they? But many of us can't figure out how to squeeze them into our schedules. Peter Drucker, an expert in management and business leadership, said that adding good ideas to our existing list of things to do is not the answer. As he concluded a seminar on leadership, he asked, "What will you *stop* doing as a result of what you have learned today?"

Our first task is to identify the nonessentials in our lives, to root them out, and then to replace them with essentials.

Another way to pose this issue is to ask: "What 20 percent of what you are doing now will you stop doing this year because it is less than effective, and what new enterprises will you launch instead?" Very few of us can make sweeping changes in our lives, but identifying and eliminating 20 percent of our nonessential activities is an excellent start.

Leaders are magnetic.

A former Prime Minister of France once said, "If you are doing big things, you attract big people. If you are doing little things, you attract little people." Leaders attract other leaders. Visionaries attract people who share their vision. People who care attract other compassionate people. Leaders are magnetic and attract others because we all want to be around people who have a zest for life and who are making a difference.

Modeling is immensely powerful—for good or ill. Good and godly leaders have an amazing impact on those around them. Paul was tough as nails, but his love was so evident that grown men wept when he told them they would never see him again. His example of love and strength was so powerful that those he left behind built churches and expanded the kingdom of God all over the known world.

Driven, demanding, dominating leaders leave a wake of broken lives as their legacies. Lethargy and boredom also have an influence as they are replicated in the complacent lives of followers. Every person in leadership is leaving a legacy. As Max Dupree wrote in his book, *Leadership Is an Art,* "Leadership is a way of thinking about institutional heirs, a way of thinking about stewardship as contrasted with ownership."

Incremental change sounds attractive at first because it promises far less pain than may be incurred when you risk sweeping changes. But incrementalism leaves a legacy of small dreams, small faith, and stunted leaders. Enthusiasm is the antidote to incremental change. It is magnetic. I'm not condoning wild promises and crazy ideas, but I fully endorse men and women whose lives have been changed by an encounter with the good-

> *But incremental-ism leaves a legacy of small dreams, small faith, and stunted leaders.*

ness and greatness of God, whose hearts are broken by the needs of people around them, and who want to use every ability, skill, and resource they possess to accomplish God's purposes. Such people won't settle for incremental growth. They dream great dreams and trust God to accomplish all he is willing to do through them.

Leaders are authentic.

Richard Baxter was a 16th-century Puritan pastor known for his intense love for God and his powerful influence on other pastors. Baxter lived with a physical condition that brought him constant pain, but the people of his English parish knew he cared deeply for him. It was said that when he first got to his parish there were no Christians, but when he left there were no unbelievers. His love for God and his love for people were unquestioned. He taught that authenticity is a primary prerequisite for winning a hearing in order to change lives. He wrote, "Men will never cast off their dearest pleasures upon the dreary request of someone who doesn't even seem to mean what he says."

I'm attracted to leaders who have the courage and maturity to talk about their own journeys. At Willow Creek conferences, Bill Hybels regularly tells as much about his failures as his successes. In fact, the failures provide the backdrop and context for the decisions that led to many of his successes.

Being authentic doesn't require that we tell every deep and dark secret to our congregation or small group. Many things should be left to God and/or a mentor. But we need to share at least some of our heartbreaks and some of our foibles for the same reason Hybels does, to provide significance for how God got our attention and how he led us in a different direction. People in our pews, classes, and groups long to understand how they, too, can learn from their mistakes. Honesty and optimism provides that example for them.

Authenticity is one of the most attractive qualities of a leader. It is a characteristic that is both winsome and powerful. Those who follow an authentic leader believe he is trustworthy because he wrestles with the same things they do. He learns from his mistakes and grows in that fertile mixture of sunlight and manure. He's not perfect, but he has a track record of courage, integrity, and growth. A church leader is a regular person who has been called to a higher standard because he or she is an example to the people of God. Authenticity, honesty and integrity win a hearing and inspire the hearer.

Nonnegotiables

Recently a friend asked me, "What are a few things you focus on as you build leaders? What are the essentials?" There are many important principles and practices of leadership development, but a few are nonnegotiable in our ministry: benchmarking, shared experiences, stimulating ideas, and training.

To begin with, I am a firm believer of "benchmarking": going to other churches to watch, to ask questions, and to experience what God is doing there. We have much to learn from one another. Any investment of time and money to feast your heart and mind on God's work in another church or organization is almost always worth the expense toward your own development and the future of your church.

When we travel to other churches, we often find that God is incredibly creative. He works in ways that we would never have imagined. We don't replicate every style of ministry we see, but God uses many of those experiences to broaden our understanding of the work of his Spirit and cause us to appreciate the beautiful mosaic of ministry in churches across the world. Then we can celebrate God's creativity and others' faithfulness to the vision he has given them.

Sharing experiences, a second nonnegotiable, is one of the most effective ways to develop leaders on a local level—especially men. Go somewhere together. Hunt, fish, bowl, play basketball. Do something physical. Get involved in projects to accomplish specific purposes. Men's hearts bond when they are doing things together. Women don't need activity to bond. If you put a group of women in a room for an hour, they will know each other's life stories. If you put a group of men in a room for an hour, they may not even know each other's names when the hour is over, but they will have talked about their hobbies and sports—and may have even figured out a way to get television reception into the room!

Expose people to stimulating ideas. This third nonnegotiable is the content component of leadership development. At every leadership meeting and during every appointment with people on our leadership team, I want to impart an idea, a concept, or a stimulating thought that captures their minds and expands their concept of God and real life.

Your ideas may be theological, sociological, or ministry oriented, but they all have a purpose behind them. Ask questions, present opposing views, and listen carefully. Use this exercise to teach people to think, as well as to grasp the particular concept.

My fourth nonnegotiable is training. One of my tasks as a leader is to think through the goals for leadership development and orchestrate a curriculum to achieve the content component. Many excellent books are available that provide a template for reflection and discussion. I trust many churches will use this book in that way.

I also want to create an environment in which our leaders support and stimulate each other. Some organizations focus on one-on-one discipleship. That's great, but they miss a powerful dynamic created through small group interaction. Others use their leadership times for administration rather than for vision, direction, development, and multiplication. Creating a leadership development environment takes forethought and planning, but it pays huge dividends. Again, you don't have to re-create the wheel. Many wonderful tools are readily available to give you a number of good options to get started.

Some churches are too focused on content. They believe that taking their leaders through a curriculum takes care of development. A good curriculum is an important part, but is only a first step. Interaction and active implementation are just as necessary for adequate training, and indeed, many people learn far more in relationships or in active service than in classrooms. Another flaw in many churches is that leadership development happens by accident. If the pastor has never seen a good model, he might try one method after another. Occasionally he will hit on something that succeeds; other times he will neglect to do anything at all that develops his people. Balance and good planning are essential to prevent these flaws from sabotaging the leadership development your church requires.

At our church, we spend a disproportionate amount of money on training our people. God has called me to help people develop so that if and when they leave our church's leadership team, their lives will have been enriched. They will have a proficiency or a sense of direction they didn't have before. If someone works directly for me at the church,

I want the person to be able to get a better job and accomplish more because he or she learned new skills and achieved higher competency than ever before. This is my goal for the custodian and the secretary as well as the assistant pastor.

Benchmarking. Shared experiences. Stimulating ideas. Training. When these things become nonnegotiable in your church, leaders rise from your ranks prepared with the creativity, maturity, and experience necessary for effective ministry.

Reflection

1. What does it mean that "everyone's a 10"?

   List four people you work with. What is the "10" area for each one?

2. Evaluate to what extent this statement is true for you: The top 20 percent of your abilities and gifts accomplish 80 percent of God's design for you.

3. Rate your influence on others from 0 (none) to 10
    (Jesus couldn't do better) according to the following
    leadership criteria:

    ___ Leaders are learners.   ___ Leadership produces
    ___ Leaders are visionaries.   change in other leaders.
    ___ Leadership involves   ___ Leaders are magnetic.
        risks.   ___ Leaders are authentic.

4. Which of the previous characteristics is your strongest?
    What can you do to maximize your impact in that area?

5. Which of the previous characteristics needs the most
    attention? What can you do to improve in that area?

6. What are specific things you can do for your leaders to:
    . . . take them or send them to be stimulated by other
    ministries?

    . . . create shared experiences among them?

    . . . expose them to stimulating ideas?

    . . . create a supportive team environment?

    . . . train them in concepts, strategy, and skills?

chapter 9

Strategy #5: Multiply Your Impact

"I tell you the truth, anyone who has faith in me will do what I have been doing. He will do even greater things than these, because I am going to the Father. And I will do whatever you ask in my name, so that the Son may bring glory to the Father" *(John 14:12-13).*

Jesus had just told his disciples (again) that he was going to die. For many months, they had assumed he was going to usher in the kingdom of God, and they were expecting to be his cabinet. But instead of power, riches, and honor, the realization was sinking in that their plans and dreams were being shattered. They would be fugitives in a few hours. That wasn't what they had planned!

Their minds must have swirled during this final dinner with Jesus, but he comforted them: "Do not let your hearts be troubled. Trust in God; trust also in me." He corrected misconceptions held by Thomas and Philip, and he gave them clear directions to keep doing what they had seen him do. The disciples' faithfulness in action, he assured them, was a sure sign of their trust in him.

His instruction was to "do what I have been doing." Surely they wondered what he meant. They had seen him trusting the Father and blending outreach with leadership development. He wanted them to keep doing that, even after he was gone. So far, so good. But Jesus didn't stop there. He then made the astounding statement that they would accomplish "even greater things." This must have set

their minds spinning! Did he mean greater things than raising the dead, healing lepers, and turning fast food lunches
into banquets for thousands?

As it turned out, that's not what Jesus meant at all.
Rather, he meant that after he returned to the Father, the
Holy Spirit would dwell in each of his followers. Then the
work of faithful people involved in the powerful blend of
outreach and leadership development would have a multiplied impact. This phenomenon of Christ producing "even
greater things" occurs at a personal level as well as an institutional level.

The Personal Level

Making a good and godly impact doesn't happen by
magic. It occurs in the context of relationships, frequently
taught as one person observes another. Paul instructed
Timothy: "And the things you have heard me say in the
presence of many witnesses entrust to reliable men who will
also be qualified to teach others" (II Tim 2:2).

Paul rarely ministered alone. He usually had one or
more people with him for mutual encouragement whom he
would help develop as leaders. Timothy had been with Paul
in all kinds of situations as he traveled to preach the gospel
and establish churches. (In fact, Paul lists Timothy as coau-
thor of six of his letters in the New Testament.) The great
apostle understood the dynamics of multi-level marketing
long before it became a popular form of business expansion.
He saw clearly that one person being faithful to God's calling simply isn't enough. Each person needs to replicate
himself or herself as many times as possible so that a multitude of "reliable" people are passionate about Christ,
gripped with the needs of people, and skilled in expanding
the kingdom of God.

One of the best examples of a multiplied impact is Chuck Smith, founder of the Calvary Chapel movement. Today you can find hundreds, and perhaps thousands, of people across the country who say, "My encounter with Jesus Christ, my call to ministry, and the cultivation of my vision and training have come through Chuck Smith's ministry." Smith has a powerful legacy. He is an "apostolic" leader whose purpose and methods of leadership development are the foundations of a genuine movement. It's easy to look at his ministry today and think, "Well, yeah. He has all kinds of resources he can use to shape young leaders." But Smith built leaders long before he built a movement. He excelled at training men and women when he was the pastor of a single church.

We don't have to have huge churches or organizations to multiply our impact. In fact, it is my guess that more young people are called to ministry out of small churches than large ones simply because they received individual attention, shepherding, and training in the small church environment. As churches grow, too many pastors become absorbed in managing the bureaucracy instead of continuing to spend quality time pouring their lives into faithful people.

I've talked to many faithful and dedicated pastors about the calling to multiply our impact, and they look at me in confusion. Some ask, "Am I not already doing this? I spend time every week with deacons and elders. I lead meetings ad nauseum. Is this what you're talking about? If it is, there's something wrong because I sure don't think I'm multiplying my impact very much. After spending years with some of these people, they still don't get it."

Committee meetings and business agendas are of only limited value in fulfilling the vision of II Timothy 2:2. Many pastors spread out their efforts and sprinkle a little attention on a lot of people instead of targeting a few. Look at the life of Christ. Out of the multitudes, some followed him. From those, he called twelve to be his disciples. Of those twelve, he spent the most time with three: Peter, James, and John. All of us need to ask, "Who are our Peter, James, and John?" Those few are the ones we need to pour our hearts and lives into. We can't invest our lives into a group of deacons and elders to the same extent that we can focus on one, two, or three people.

Some might read these words and say, "But isn't that showing preference? How will others respond when they realize I'm spending more time with someone else?" Good question. Jesus' example is that he showed love to all, but selected three to be with him in the most tender and intimate circumstances. That's his example, and it is one he wants us to follow.

A genuine commitment to multiply your impact in the lives of a few leaders requires two essential choices: the selection of the right people, and the rigorous reorientation of your schedule to make sure you focus your time and energies on this crucial responsibility. Don't settle for any warm body, and don't make your selection too quickly. Ask God to lead you to the person or people he has chosen for you. Jesus prayed all night before he selected the Twelve. Perhaps you and I could pray for an hour or two at least as we seek God's guidance.

The Lord may lead you to talk to someone you wouldn't have considered. Be obedient to his Spirit's prompting and have an honest conversation with that person. Don't feel rushed to make an offer of long-term commitment to discipleship in the first discussion. Tell the person what you are considering, and ask questions to find out what God has been putting on that person's heart. Ask if he or she has considered a stronger commitment to follow Christ, and leave the meeting with a commitment that both of you will pray. (By the way, at this level of leadership development, avoid mixed gender groups. Men should mentor men, and women should mentor women.)

I heartily recommend that you form a small group, just like Jesus did, so each of you can benefit from the insights and zeal of the group. Another way to select wisely is to meet with people for a month or two to address short-term training goals. This allows you to see if your candidates respond faithfully to your leadership. If they do, then you can take the next step by offering a more permanent relationship. If not, the short-term commitment can end gracefully. It is far better to take extra time at the beginning to select wisely than to jump too quickly and realize that you have made a strong commitment to someone who is a poor choice.

A second essential is to organize your schedule to make room for this kind of mentoring. Don't make the mistake of trying to add this commitment to an already busy schedule. If imparting your life to a few is important (and I believe it is a biblical mandate of leadership), then step back to analyze what you are doing now. Carve out sufficient time, not only for one-on-one and small group meetings with your Timothys, but also for prayer and preparation so you will have a deep reservoir of knowledge and skills to draw from.

Every church has at least a few men and women, young or not-so-young, who want to be mentored in a significant way. One of the first people I mentored was a vice president of human resources in a large corporation who felt called to play a leadership role in our church. I was an associate pastor when asked me to disciple him. I felt a little awkward at first because I was only 26 years old and he was about 35, but he wasn't deterred by my misgivings. We made a commitment to meet every Thursday morning for a year. I told him I'd teach and show him everything I'd ever learned about leadership if he would teach me about personnel. It was a wonderful year! I learned a lot about selection and placement of people in organizations, and he became a dynamic leader in the church.

My experience as a wet-behind-the-ears mentor taught me several important lessons:

— Sometimes we select our Timothys, but sometimes they select us. We need to be open and receptive to the Lord's surprises.

— We can't manufacture passion for Christ in a mentor/disciple relationship. If the enthusiasm isn't there to begin with, the person isn't a viable candidate. Instead, we need to look for an existing spark that God will fan into a flame.

— Multiplying my impact took concentrated time and attention. We met together every Thursday morning, even when it was inconvenient. Both of us could have filled up that time with other things, but we made it a priority.

— A mentoring relationship is not one-way. I learned as much from my "disciple" as he did from me. I believe my openness to him and my appreciation for his skills and abilities gave us a far stronger, deeper, and warmer relationship than if I had seen him merely as "a project" to attend to.

Good leadership requires a strong blend of gentle love, like a nursing mother, and toughness, like a soldier. This blend begins with the very selection of disciples. Not everyone who says, "I want to be your Timothy," is ready for the investment of your time and attention. John Mark's failure, whatever it was, caused Paul to veto his participation on the next trip. Was Paul being unforgiving and ungracious? Not at all. He was being a steward of his time and the calling of

God. Later, after John Mark had proven himself, Paul again sought his help in ministry.

The strategy of "leadership development by committee meetings" doesn't work. Some churches enjoy dabbling in the latest business-world leadership techniques and fads that promise growth. The pattern we see in the Scriptures, however, is that growth is a direct result of rich relationships in which we impart love, hope, insight, and skills to a few, who then will be able to pass along those traits to still more people. We need to get out of the business-as-usual mindset of managing our churches. We need to make a sure and strong commitment to multiply our impact by following the same pattern of Paul and Jesus through prayer, discernment, careful selection, imparting skills, and releasing well-trained people for ministry.

> *The pattern we see in the Scriptures, however, is that growth is a direct result of rich relationships in which we impart love, hope, insight, and skills to a few, who then will be able to pass along those traits to still more people.*

The Institutional Level

Peter Wagner said that church planting is the single most effective method of evangelism in the world today. His research shows this phenomenon to be statistically verifiable in churches across America, including the Southern Baptist Convention, which is known for its emphasis on evangelism. The ratio of members to new converts in an existing church is ten times higher than in a church plant. The reason for this is simple: It is the law of inertia. Existing churches focus much of their energy on managing the status quo and meeting needs of the members.

The heart and soul of new churches is outreach in the community. The reason they were started in the first place was to take the gospel to those who are unchurched. These facts don't absolve existing churches from having a stronger emphasis on evangelism. However, they demonstrate that overcoming inertia in an existing church requires a paradigm shift from business-as-usual management to a vision that blends cutting-edge outreach with effective leadership development.

Every leader and every church in tune with God's heart has a missions mindset. We often think of a missionary as a nerdy person who lives in the jungle, wears a grass skirt, swabs sores, and eats weird things. But the entire planet is now our mission field, from the most hardened and antagonistic Muslim nation to the chatty neighbor next door. We can export some of our best and brightest to minister in foreign lands, but we can also have a missions mindset as we reach people by planting churches in communities nearby. The Great Commission is to be fulfilled in Jerusalem, in Judea and Samaria, and to the ends of the earth. As we go to the ends of the earth, let's not forget our hometowns.

When we started our church in Carson Valley, Nevada, we regularly received phone calls from people asking, "Why would you start a church here? Everyone here already goes to church." (Our research showed us that only five percent were churched!) Existing churches often question the wisdom and effectiveness of expending the effort and energy required to start yet another new church. In light of their existing circumstances, the new endeavor seems beyond the realm of reason. Entrepreneurs experience this phenomenon in new business ventures. People often ask them, "Why would you want to do *that?*"

And yet, the Great Commission compels us to reach the unreached. According to the American Society for Church Growth, no county in America has more people in churches today than 10 years ago. (Here in Carson Valley, we're challenging that statistic!) Churches with vision and a heart for the lost are needed in every community in America. In my work as a denominational executive, and especially as the pastor of a church plant, the Lord has clarified the process of starting new churches. Here are eleven steps to help any group of believers plant a new church or any existing church to replicate itself. (For more information on these and other church planting resources, visit VisionQuest Ministries at www.vqresources.com).

Step 1: Uphold a clear and well-processed vision.

Make sure you begin with a clear vision that has come from the throne of God. If you don't have a clear idea of what to do with the crowd when it comes, you will be in trouble! This vision has to be prayed through and communicated to people who will join the leadership team of the new church.

Step 2: Lay out an aggressive plan of action, including a fundraising plan.

Tremendous resources are available to help you develop your action plan. Four recommendations are:

- *Purpose Driven Church Planting Materials* (www.purposedriven.com)
- *Dynamic Church Planting* (Paul Becker, 619-749-9347)
- *Church Planter's Toolkit* (Bob Logan & Steve Ogne, Church Resource Ministries)
- *Planting Thriving New Churches* (Ray Johnston, www.baysideonline.com)

I have found that church planters tend to underestimate the amount of money required to successfully plant a new

Raise funds from those who "buy into" your vision because of God's work in their lives through your ministry.

church. They also overestimate the amount that a denominational agency, mother church, or sponsor should give them at the launch. Go to people who have been impacted by your ministry. They will support your vision. Raise funds from those who "buy into" your vision because of God's work in their lives through your ministry.

Step 3: Create a "people pathway" for assimilation.

Assimilation at every level of involvement revolves around connecting people in relationships and service. Articulating a clear plan at the start helped people on our leadership team have confidence about where we were heading. Rick Warren's model at Saddleback is the most helpful in our setting.[21] We changed Warren's visual paradigm from a baseball diamond to a triangle with the words Attract, Attach, and Activate.[22]

Over time we have "morphed" our own ministry structures in order to focus on "Visitors," "Attenders," and "Leaders." Some of the processes and activities for assimilation are different at each numerical level, but they still focus on connecting people in relationships and ministry.

Step 4: Keep your church planting plans flexible and be open to unexpected opportunities.

We had some great plans on paper—and some of them even worked! Others didn't. We recorded thirteen 60-second

21 See *The Purpose Driven Church,* specifically "Part Five: Building Up the Church."
22 See Chapter 5 in this book.

commercials for radio spots, but we got zero response from them, and direct mailing in our area didn't prove to be nearly as effective as we hoped. But we discovered some great strategies that did fit our area: local public access television and newspaper inserts.

My brother Gene is a marketing genius, and many of our early inserts are classics! We remained flexible and finally got a very positive response from the unchurched community.

Step 5: Prayerfully seek godly core leaders and key ministry leaders.

Implosion—falling apart from within—is a potential danger for church plants. Churches that attract crowds without first building a leadership base to care for them will be handicapped from the start. Look for gifted, enthusiastic leaders to become part of your launch team. Work with them to cultivate a game plan for how the church will "go public" with specific ministries: children, youth, music, etc.

Step 6: Hold preview services three to six months prior to your launch service, and build your core group to 100 adults or more.

At each preview service, we tried to approximate the styles and levels of music, children's ministry, and teaching we felt we could attain by Launch Sunday. We challenged people who attended the preview services to receive Christ as Savior and to consider becoming part of the Carson Valley Christian Launch Team. Each preview service added 20 or more people to our launch team!

Step 7: Engage people in ministries, discovery classes, small groups, and Bible studies.

After each preview service, we helped people move through the process of attaching and activating their participation with us. That same afternoon we offered Discovery 101, a class in which I explained the gospel and the vision of our church. In hindsight, this was a great move. People who were energized by the Sunday morning program often came out of curiosity to participate in Discovery 101.

During the five months leading up to our public launch in February 1998, we connected people to ministries, discovery classes, and small groups. This period was key to the success of our launch. I strongly advocate taking enough time to do a good job of making these strategic connections.

Step 8: Identify the core group as your "Launch Team," create job descriptions, and prepare for the launch.

By the time of our official launch date, 65 of our 100 adults had been through Discovery 301 and were serving in ministry. We had identified specific roles and everyone had a sense of what it would take to start our church. We set this pattern of involvement at the beginning, and it is now firmly embedded in our church's DNA.

Step 9: Create excellent publicity, especially two months before launch.

My brother Gene developed publicity to build public interest and invite people to make a specific response. First we built a theme, "The Next Great Day in History," that focused on our launch date. We followed it up with a second phase of publicity focusing on a teaching series entitled "Winning Big in the Game of Life."

We involved our people in our publicity by giving them fold-over, wallet-sized cards and encouraging them to canvass neighborhoods and local businesses. We wanted to create a "buzz" of activity in our area. By the time we launched, we had created a "big event" mentality.

Evangelism is in the center of our vision. George Barna believes that as many as 40 percent of the people who visit your church come because you host special events.

Step 10: Plan a super launch, and go public with the things you'd die for.

You can't control everything. Mistakes happen. Weather turns bad and people get sick, but you can decide what you are "going to the wall" for. In our case, we decided to focus on three things:

- Relevant biblical messages;
- Upbeat, contemporary music; and
- An excellent children's ministry.

These three distinctives have remained our "crowd" focus to this day. We built our launch as big as possible. We have 100,000 people in our 30-mile focus area, so we got about half of one percent of our target population to attend our launch. Since then we have doubled that total and have one percent of our target population attending each week—with plenty more people yet to reach! How you start impacts your ministry more than you can imagine. Begin well!

Step 11: Go for it! Affirm your leadership team and practice "continuous improvement."

Spend lots of time affirming your leadership team. Be a positive person from the platform, and challenge them to "continuous improvement" inspired by Philippians 4:13. Build a culture of affirmation *and* expectation. God is good . . . all the time! All the time . . . God is good!

> *Spend lots of time affirming your leadership team.*

God is sovereign. It is his church. You are accountable for the gifts and resources he has entrusted to you, but he is the one who causes the growth. God will accomplish things far beyond your imagination, and you will see a 30- or 60- or 100-fold return from sowing the seed of his word.

As we look at the ministries of Jesus and Paul, their lives were characterized by a few essentials: abject, complete commitment to the Father's purpose and will; joy and passion in serving the Father; and a powerful blend of outreach and leadership development. As they trained leaders, they multiplied their impact by selecting wisely, imparting themselves wholeheartedly, and releasing people to change the world. That's our task, too.

Reflection

1. Who has had the most powerful, positive impact on you? How did that person impart the love and life of Christ to you, believe in you, equip you, etc.?

2. Do you have a "Timothy" (or two or three) whom you are discipling? Describe how and why you are imparting love, hope, insights, and skills to such people.

3. What are some good ways to select people wisely?

4. Look at your schedule and determine when, where, and how you can have a Paul/Timothy relationship with one or more people. What will you have to give up to make this work? What preparation needs to be done? What will you and they gain?

5. Describe the most successful church plant you have participated in.

6. Describe your church's (and your personal) vision and commitment for church planting.

7. Write a brief analysis of the eleven steps in this chapter. Which ones seem especially important? Which ones seem the easiest to achieve?

8. Is church planting a viable part of your strategic plan? Why or why not? If not, how could it be implemented?

10 "A Vision without a Plan . . ."

"Since ancient times no one has heard,
no ear has perceived,
no eye has seen any God besides you,
who acts on behalf of those who wait for
him" (Is 64:4).

This is not a book on planning. It is a book on vision and strategy, yet planning is essential to fulfill the dream God has given you and your church. I believe God is ready, willing, and able to accomplish far more than we are seeing in our churches.

Isaiah had a sense of wonder at God's goodness and greatness in accomplishing great things, and he wrote of the importance of waiting for God. Waiting is not primarily a function of time, but of expectation. When I wait at an airport for a taxi, I fully expect one to come sooner or later. In the same way, a heart of faith that waits on God fully expects him to act according to his nature, to accomplish wonderful, marvelous things in people's lives.

God has chosen to include us in his work, and planning is an essential element in the process of building God's kingdom. We are his soldiers who plan the battle, athletes who plan our training regimen, and farmers who plan to plow, sow, water, and reap a rich harvest.

Some people are gifted planners with disciplined minds. They are creative and conceptual, and can organize a host of seemingly chaotic events and people into a seamless whole.

More Christian leaders, however, are *not* gifted in this way. They are in their position primarily because they love God and love people. Their strengths are relational, not conceptual. Therefore, wise leaders develop a team approach. Instead of being threatened by people who have strengths they don't possess, they seek out people with complementary gifts and value their contributions. When the strengths of each person are maximized, far more is accomplished.

Planning to Plan

Stephen Covey encourages people to "begin with the end in mind." The first step in planning is to have a clear vision of what we believe God wants to accomplish in and through us. Before we dive into plotting a course to implement the five strategies outlined in this book, some leaders need to back up and examine the foundation of their planning process.

A clearly articulated vision sets the course like a compass for a hiker. Leaders need to pray, study the Scriptures, talk, and pray some more to determine God's calling for their congregation. Every church is called to fulfill the Great Commandment to love God with all our hearts and the Great Commission to take the gospel to the world. But each church has its own identity, ministry philosophy, and methods of accomplishing those great goals.

In virtually every meeting, every service, every small group, and every one-on-one mentoring meeting, they need to include three components: vision, relationships, and programs.

As the ministry philosophy takes shape, the pastor and top leaders need to form their strategy to develop leaders. In virtually every meeting, every service, every small group, and every one-on-one mentoring meeting, they need to include three components: vision, relationships, and programs. Vision challenges people to believe God for more; relationships provide the warmth and modeling essential for them to hear and act on what is said; and programs provide the tracks for needs to be met. An essential ingredient in all of this is the leader's faith and optimism. No matter how difficult the obstacle, no matter how high the calling, a good leader is an example of steadfast faith in God and tenacious optimism that God will accomplish his good purposes.

Not every one who fills a slot on a church's organizational chart needs to be in the central planning group. Select people for this group who have a heart of faith and proven abilities. If you have too many "top leaders" to plan effectively, or if this group lacks a vital ingredient of wisdom or skill, invite someone with the skills you need to join the central planning group for a short time to complete the planning process. Of course, smaller churches need to select this group as carefully as larger churches. The calling and the stakes for them are just as high. Good planning requires forethought, wisdom, time, and energy. In other words, plan to plan.

Develop Good Habits of Planning

Planning is like any other skill: we can develop habits that continually better our ability to plan effectively. I want to outline several suggestions for improving our planning habits.

Continue to grow strong in your grasp of the heart of God, the needs of people, and your gifts and talents.

Vision begins with the vital combination of experiencing God and being touched by the needs of others. The abilities to pursue our vision are God-given, and we never grow beyond them. For our entire lives, they remain the heart and soul of our walks with God and our service for him. As long as we keep growing, learning, stretching, and wrestling with them, our love for God will deepen and we will become more useful to him.

I've watched some people get to a certain level of success and prominence in their lives and ministries, and they stop growing. They feel they have arrived, so they stop pressing on toward the high calling of God. We need more like Caleb, who, even though he was an old man, saw prime real estate in the Promised Land and cried, "Give me that mountain!" What was good enough for most people wasn't good enough for him.

Know yourself. Know what motivates you and what trips you up. Be a student of your "bents" in your thoughts, your family life, your moods, and your ministry—not so you can be absorbed in yourself, but so you can see trouble coming and make wise decisions. Ask people for feedback about your abilities and effectiveness. Focus your energies on your strengths. That's where your maximum effectiveness lies. But it may also be necessary to devote some time to filling holes in your leadership skills in order to be as effective as possible.

Cultivate the skill of vision-casting.

Every leader is responsible to impart personal passion for the Lord and for serving him. This must be far more than lip service. Those who are effective in imparting vision are successful because passion flows from every pore and is present in every conversation. Genuine passion cannot be contained. It will find expression in one way or another.

Words must connect with actions. If I tell you that Ford is the best truck you can buy, but I drive a Chevy, you have every reason to question my honesty and convictions. If I tell you that evangelism is a vital part of ministry but I have no personal stories to share, you won't be motivated to share your faith—and you won't be motivated to apply other truths I teach, either, because you won't trust me.

One of the most effective ways of imparting vision is taking people to see where God is working ("benchmarking"). It is an exceptionally effective way to stimulate faith and demonstrate new methodology in ministry because people actually experience the strategy and programs instead of just talking about them. Another way to impart vision is to give people resources that have stimulated your own sense of calling. A host of books, videos, tapes, CDs, websites, and other resources are available. Use these as curricula to communicate a specific ministry philosophy or to supplement particular points you want to make with your leaders.

Assess resources and count the cost.

Jesus told a couple of short parables about the importance of knowing what a commitment will cost: before taking his army into battle, a wise king determines whether he can win or not; and before beginning to build, a contractor must assess the cost in time and materials to see if he has enough to finish. Similarly, before a church leader embarks on a vision, he is wise to carefully consider the cost in people, finances, and space. Key leaders must be selected and trained, and they must fully endorse the vision. The funds, gifts, and partnerships must be in place before you begin. And finally, the facilities must be adequate to accommodate the event. All the provisions for comfort, speed of service, and effective communication must be readily available.

A fresh, dynamic vision isn't accomplished by trying to stretch your existing budget a little farther. Instead, look for new resources—both people and funds.

Don't overlook the wealth of resources in your church. A fresh, dynamic vision isn't accomplished by trying to stretch your existing budget a little farther. Instead, look for new resources—both people and funds. Trust God to stir new hearts with the vision so more people volunteer to be involved. And look for new ways to fund projects. Partnerships are a terrific asset, and people often respond very positively when asked to give to the vision of a specific program. Give them the opportunity for their lives and their money to make a difference for eternity. That's not a guilt trip. It's an open invitation to be involved in God's work.

Spend quality time with people.

With all the pressures and demands on our time, many of us now avoid deep, meaningful interaction—even those of us who used to thrive on relationships. But effective ministry revolves around rich, meaningful relationships. Look again at the life of Christ. He took people with him virtually everywhere but the cross—and actually, he took all of us there. His disciples watched him when he healed people, when the crowds loved him, when he was angry with the moneychangers, and when his heart broke in grief. He shared with them his deepest desires and his hopes for their futures. If Jesus put so much emphasis on building quality relationships, and if we are committed to "walk as he walked," we need to examine how we can adapt our schedules and priorities so people remain important to us.

Provide stories of heroes.

Meaningful relationships with people lead to rich conversations when they tell you what they really care about and how God is working in their lives. During those dialogues you can *notice* the movement of God, *name* it by pointing out how he is working, and *nurture* it with specific affirmations and encouragement. In those conversations, you find out the person's real story and you see what puts light in his eyes and fire in his heart.

Jesus knew Peter was a fisherman. When he called Peter and his brother Andrew to be disciples, he said, "Follow me, and I will make you fishers of men." Jesus connected God's sovereign purpose with Peter's experience as a fisherman, and his message moved Peter to action. The picture Christ painted for Peter captured his heart because it touched his life's patterns and passions.

In the same way, if someone told me today that I could be a concert pianist, I'd respond, "That's nice." But because I have no grasp of what that means, the prospect doesn't move me very much. On the other hand, if someone told me God's purpose for me was to help pastors and other church leaders become far more effective in fulfilling the Great Commandment and the Great Commission, I'd be thrilled. That's what I care about and what ignites my passion. (And that very vision is what drives me to write this book.) We need to know people well enough so that God can use us to connect their God-given passions with wonderful opportunities to honor Christ.

Jesus told parables and stories to move hearts. Today, good speakers still bring life to their concepts by telling great stories. My commitment is to instill life into my ministry by telling the stories of men and women, often in our own community of faith, who have trusted God and found him faithful. Such people are the heroes of our congregation and powerful motivators to others. People may come to hear me speak, but they are moved to action by a story of a person just like them (as if I'm not!) who boldly acted in faith and saw God work in his or her life. These stories are so important to our life of faith that I consider myself a steward of the life stories of our people. It is my responsibility to know and use them wisely so they have the greatest impact on others.

Sometimes great stories are not of heroes, but of shared (and sometimes very strange) experiences. In December 1997, before our church was launched, we were meeting in a casino with about 80 people in our core group. At one point, 14 people wanted to be baptized, but we didn't know how we could pull it off. We asked the casino manager for permission to conduct a baptism in our second-floor meeting room at the casino. He thought for a while, then said, "Go ahead, but don't tell me how you do it!"

We bought a used hot tub for $100, and on Saturday night my brother Gene and I loaded it in the back of his pickup and took it to the casino. We went up the back hallway, and we barely got the hot tub into the elevator. On the second floor, a fancy catered dinner was going on in the meeting room, so we rolled the hot tub end over end past the servers and the serving carts. As we did, we received a lot of strange and unhappy looks. At last we got the hot tub to the end of the hall.

The next morning we arrived at the casino at 6 A.M., attached a long garden hose to the casino's water heater, and filled up the tub. This was working out great! When we finished, we put a cover over the hot tub and waited for people to arrive at 10 o'clock. We were all set . . . we thought.

However, someone had left the back door open all morning, and it was 12 degrees outside. It was almost freezing in the hallway where the hot tub was located! When we took the lid off the hot tub, the hot water and the cold air collided, filling the hallway with steam! That day 14 people were baptized, but 80 people still talk about a "once in a lifetime experience." It was a baptism they'll never forget!

Communicate transferable principles.

I'm looking at my Bible as I write. It is large, with over a thousand pages. It was written long ago to cultures very different from ours. It seems daunting to me sometimes, and I try to imagine how its sheer volume and complexity overwhelm people who have never studied systematic theology.

I've noticed that speakers who seem to make the most profound impact on their hearers are those who can synthesize biblical concepts into transferable principles. No one can keep up with 343,643 things we have to know in order to walk with God, but many people are eager to learn and apply what they can. The most significant and transforming lessons come from umbrella principles such as forgiveness, grace, the sovereignty of God, the deity of Christ, resurrection and judgement, and ministry principles like the ones covered in these pages. A person doesn't have to be a Rhodes Scholar to understand God's purpose and ways. It is my great privilege and desire to communicate the truth of Scripture so that it changes lives, not so it fills notebooks. Great truths clearly grasped become immensely transferable. When we are excited about their impact on us, we delight in telling others.

> *Great truths clearly grasped become immensely transferable. When we are excited about their impact on us, we delight in telling others.*

Think of the pastors and teachers who have had the greatest impact on your life. Even scholars like J. I. Packer distill their research so that people like you and I can grasp it and allow the Holy Spirit to transform us with it. And ministry leaders like Rick Warren and Bill Hybels have distilled their vision and experiences into concepts that have changed the lives of millions. Our job is to follow their example, to teach transferable principles with clarity and power.

Implement the five strategies.

I wish every person reading this book would implement all five strategies completely today, but that's an unrealistic expectation. In some cases, the foundation of a clear vision needs to be established. In other cases, the leader needs to build credibility and win the trust of the people. In all cases, it takes time to build a solid group of leaders and pour your passion and philosophy into them so they are with you, heart and soul. Some of us may be farther along than others, but all of us can at least get started.

The questions and exercises at the end of each chapter are designed to help you dream big dreams, reflect on your current situation, and take concrete steps to fill in the gap between vision and current reality. Take time to wrestle with these questions, pray diligently for God's guidance, and find resources that will help you take each step in this exciting journey. Learn to combine wisdom with boldness, patience with zeal, and a good listening ear with a bold voice of vision. Plan big events that capture people's hearts and touch thousands outside your church's walls; build strong, effective partnerships with organizations in your community; help people find the place where they can serve with joy and passion; and multiply your impact by finding a Timothy or two to pour your life into. You don't have to do it all right now. But at least take the first—or the next—step.

Mark Twain said, "The secret of getting ahead is getting started. The secret of getting started is breaking your complex, overwhelming tasks into small, manageable tasks, and then starting on the first one."

Help people overcome obstacles.

In established churches, a few people respond positively and immediately to a fresh vision. Far more want to wait to see if all their questions are answered before they buy into the new program. Some won't join the parade until they actually see the program working and the benefits are proven. And of course, you can always find a few stodgy codgers who still don't think ice cream will catch on.

I welcome honest questions. Our church is young and many of our members are young believers, so questions are natural. For us, the most common questions arise not because someone wants to cling to the way things used to be, but instead because our people don't yet understand the biblical directives and our ministry philosophy. I'm very happy to explain those things to them as long as they will listen, and I'm happy to give them tangible examples as long as they will watch.

Yet people may ask questions for very different reasons. Some sincerely doubt whether a new direction will work, perhaps because they've been in churches that tried to change and experienced failure for some reason. Or someone may doubt the integrity of the leader. People with these kinds of questions usually aren't swayed by eloquence or passionate verbiage. At best, they will hold their criticism until the leaders have had a chance to prove themselves. That's all you can ask, and that's all you'll probably get.

In an existing church, I always assume some people will be adamantly against any significant change in the early going. But I also assume that many, if not most of them, will get on board after the first signs of genuine success. That gives a leader hope, and it keeps him or her from becoming defensive and argumentative. People, contrary to what some church leaders believe, are not the enemy. Most of them dearly love God and want him to be honored in the church. But they've been burned before by poor leadership, and they certainly don't intend to get burned again. Be patient with them, explain your heart and your purposes, and ask them to pray for you as you move forward.

A very real obstacle for many in the business world is that they don't see how God can use their abilities for his glory. They have segmented the sacred and the secular, and they believe what they do every day is at best meaningless, and at worst a hindrance to their faith.

I recently began working with a graphic artist who had never worked for a church before. She has spent years designing promotional materials to sell soap and cars, but now she is excited because she can use her skills to touch people's lives for Christ. She puts far more effort and heart in what she does for me than in her other work, and, I trust, she gets far more out of it.

> *It is my role to help people build bridges between their everyday worlds and the kingdom of God.*

Author and theologian John R. W. Stott said, "It is the task of the preacher in the modern world to hold the Bible in one hand, the newspaper in the other, and build a bridge between the two."[23] It is my role to help people build bridges between their everyday worlds and the kingdom of God.

Get some quick wins for people.

John Maxwell says that leaders need to create "wins" for their people. In their excellent book, *The Leadership Challenge,* James Kouzes and Barry Posner tell the story of Don Bennett, the first amputee to reach the summit of Mount Rainier, near Seattle. On his first attempt, he got within 410 feet of the summit when a violent wind almost blew him off the mountain. During the next year, Bennett worked out and got himself in even better shape. When he was ready, he made his second attempt. After five grueling days, he reached the top. After the climb, Bennett was asked, "How did you do it?" He replied, "One hop at a

---

23   John R. W. Stott, *Between Two Worlds: The Challenge of Preaching Today,* (Wm. B. Eerdmans, Grand Rapids, Michigan, 1994), p. 140.

time. I imagined myself on top of that mountain 1000 times a day. But when I started to climb it, I just said to myself, 'Anybody can hop from here to there.' And I would. And when the going got roughest, and I was really exhausted, that's when I would look down at the path ahead and say to myself, 'You just have to take one more step, and anybody can do that.' And I would." The authors comment, "The most effective change processes are incremental; they break down big problems into small, doable steps and get a person to say yes numerous times, not just once."[24]

One of the most profitable things I've done as a shepherd of God's flock is to encourage young believers to grow. I create situations so they can see successes early in their Christian lives. That means we may have to work like crazy to involve young Christians (whatever their ages may be) in helping us host big events. But at the end of the day, I can honestly tell them, "Wow! Look what God did today, and you played a vital role in making it happen."

The Scriptures are clear that we aren't to put immature believers in leadership positions, and that's not what I'm talking about at all. Any believer can be a greeter, flip hamburgers, put up promotional material, paint signs, put out chairs, host a booth, or serve in countless other ways. Invite people to be a part of something that will change lives. They will love it! And young believers don't know any better— they may just tell somebody how they trusted Christ!

Don't Stop Growing

Dee Hock, author of *The Chaordic Organization*, which describes the close connection between chaos and order in any group, suggests that 50 to 60 percent of a leader's time

---

24 James Kouzes and Barry Posner, *The Leadership Challenge*, (Jossey-Bass, San Francisco, 1995), pp. 242-244.

should be spent in self-management. That may sound ridiculous to some of us, but the principle is sound. We can't give away something we don't possess. Too many of us, about 70 percent in my estimation, try to impart passion for Christ and ministry although ours dried up long ago. When the well is empty, nobody can drink. If we are empty, the best we can do is adopt someone else's vision and present it as ours. We won't really own it.

Fill up the well. Replenish the aquifer that feeds the springs and wells in your own life. When we are excited about what God is doing in our own lives, we are excited about what God is doing—and what he wants to do—in others' lives. Vision for the church springs from a heart full of God.

Do you remember what it was like when you were excited about a truth or a concept the Lord taught you? That kind of enthusiasm changes lives and proves the integrity of a leader who is giving away what he possesses. It's the stuff of life and ministry.

Reflection

1. Are you gifted in planning? Why or why not? Who are some people around you who could complement your abilities so you can plan more effectively?

2. What does it mean to "plan to plan"? How can you do this effectively?

3. Evaluate the current status and your plans to plan in order to:
   - Continue to grow strong in your grasp of the heart of God, the needs of people, and your gifts and talents.

   - Cultivate the skill of vision-casting.

   - Assess resources and count the cost.

   - Spend quality time with people.

   - Provide stories of heroes.

- Communicate transferable principles.

- Implement the five strategies.

- Help people overcome obstacles.

- Get some quick wins for people.

4. Describe how you will complete your planning process to prioritize, gather resources, and implement these plans.

11 *Keep It Fresh*

"For what is our hope, our joy, or the crown in which we will glory in the presence of our Lord Jesus when he comes? Is it not you? Indeed, you are our glory and joy" (I Thess 2:19).

*E*very church has its own identity in fulfilling its purpose to reach out to the lost and build men and women of faith, led by those who love Christ with all their hearts and are committed to do anything—anything!—to honor him. But any church whose identity is to "sit, soak, and sour" has gotten off track and is missing out on what God has in store for its people.

A friend and I were talking about this subject, and he said, "But John, my church's identity is to be a place that avoids risk at all costs. That's how the leaders hope to keep people coming. They want it to be safe. They don't want to challenge anybody to trust God for great things."

Every church has a central gift mix or skill set, and an identifiable style of ministry, but those are not the fundamental issues. At the core of the church and the leadership is their grasp of the heart of God. If a church isn't gripped by the heart of God, I'd rather it not try to implement any of the strategies in this book. I would much rather those people be reached by Christians who genuinely love God and people. Jesus had some pretty harsh words for a church he defined as lukewarm. It's far better to be cold or hot than to be tepid in our response to the incredible grace and greatness of Almighty God.

God's grand design for us is not to be safe. It is to take risks to reach people, to leave 99 sheep to search for the one who went astray, to sweep the house looking for a single lost coin, to sell everything we have and count everything as worthless rubbish compared to the surpassing value of knowing and following Jesus Christ.

I've spoken in many churches over the years. In some of them, I preached my heart out, but the impact was like a Randy Johnson fastball hitting a huge pillow. A soft thump, then back to normal. But I've also spoken in churches where the leaders were so passionate about Christ that their enthusiasm had infected the entire congregation. Sometimes my messages weren't all that profound, but the look on people's faces told me they were absorbing every syllable. They reminded me of a line in a song by the popular Christian group, Caedmon's Call, that prays to God, "Send down Your word. We are eager to hear it." Man, I love to be with people who are eager to hear the word of God and ready to take action on what they hear!

If we are not stirred by the prospect of reaching people for Christ with the most amazing message and power the world has ever known, we need to step back and take stock of our hearts. Some of us may need to look again at Catherine Marshall's prayer at the end of Chapter 3 and make her prayer our own.

Keep Your Calling Fresh

A fundamental law of nature is that life tends toward randomness. This concept is called entropy. Rocks erode into dust and are swept away. Maple seeds are blown by the wind in a random, scattered pattern. We see it all around us. A fundamental law of organizations is that bureaucracy increases with growth and time, which is why entrepreneurs are like a breath of fresh air! Churches and other groups begin to spend more time in administration, meetings, and maintaining the existing programs. They spend less time and energy on the cutting-edge activities that gave them life and growth to begin with.

Paul planted many churches on his missionary journeys. He could have focused his energies on staying longer in each place and solving more of their problems. He might even have become the first denominational exec, but he kept his calling fresh. Even a casual reading of his first letter to the Christians at Thessalonica shows that he didn't allow growth and multiplied needs to get him off track. Take some time to read just the first couple of chapters and you'll see Paul's tenacity to "dare to tell you (Christ's) gospel in spite of strong opposition" (2:2). His motivation was only and always to please God, not to please people (2:3-6).

Paul's relationships were rich and warm, not characterized by distant formality. In one of the most tender statements in all of his letters, he told them, "We loved you so much that we were delighted to share with you not only the gospel of God but our lives as well, because you had become dear to us" (2:8). His care was like a nursing mother (2:7), and his powerful love like a father (2:11). He told them he longed to see them again, and he called them his "glory and joy" (2:17-20). Paul kept his calling fresh by not allowing himself to be a victim of creeping bureaucracy that absorbs our time and rots our souls. Even when the churches grew and administrative needs multiplied, Paul made sure he stayed true to his love for Christ, his ministry of outreach, and the power of deep, affirming relationships.

Paul kept his calling fresh by not allowing himself to be a victim of creeping bureaucracy that absorbs our time and rots our souls.

203

Creeping bureaucracy is so prevalent because it looks attractive in some ways. It promises a position of respect and safety from risks. *If we are in love with what is, we won't be willing to sacrifice for what could be.* Organizational inertia is one of the most significant hindrances to gaining and fulfilling God's vision. Many of us are too much in love with positions, status, and safe layers provided by bureaucracy. I've noticed that in my 23 years of ministry, the movement of God is almost always *in spite of* my position, not *because* of it. Position promises safety; vision demands risks.

When God has prompted me to dream big dreams for him, I've had to ask myself, "Am I willing to step out of the known into the unknown, from safety to risk, from a stable position to trust God to provide for me out on a limb?" Order is not the highest goal in the life of an individual or an organization. Vitality is.

Keep Your View of God Fresh

One of the great benefits of sharing the gospel with unbelievers is that we get to see God's grace from their perspective. They aren't steeped in theology like we are. The gospel message hasn't become stale to them like it can to us. They are amazed that the Creator of the universe would come to earth, die a horrible death, and be raised from the dead—because he loves them personally! Their wide eyes always encourage me to look at the God of the Scriptures in fresh ways.

One of the most astounding passages in the New Testament is John's account of Jesus in the early chapters of Revelation. John was perhaps Jesus' most intimate friend. He was the one who rested his head on Jesus' chest at the Last Supper and who identified himself in his gospel as "the disciple whom Jesus loved." They were very, very close. But when the risen Christ appeared to John in his glory, John was blown away. He described Christ as a figure of dazzling light, with his eyes blazing with fire, his feet glowing, and his voice thundering like a roaring waterfall. Out of his mouth came a sharp two-edged sword, and "his face was like the sun shining in all its brilliance" (1:16). Although John was one of Jesus' best friends on earth, when he witnessed the sight, he "fell at his feet as though dead." Jesus, ever the tender as well as awesome God, touched his friend and reassured him of his love, his power, and his purpose.

When I think of Jesus, do I think of him as a stiff image in stained glass or perhaps a pitiful but noble person who suffered for others? Or is he someone so awesome that he blows me away? If the Messiah has become commonplace to us, our worship quickly turns into work and our glad service into bondage. Instead of being in awe of his greatness and grace, we merely go through the motions of our respectable positions of church leadership.

All of us experience times of dryness and darkness. We wrestle with our sinful natures, the world's pressures, and an implacable enemy who is committed to deceiving and discouraging us any way he can. We won't experience completely pure motives and total relief from these attacks until we see Christ face to face, but our task until then is to keep pursuing him through thick and thin. God has given us a deep, unquenchable thirst for him, and nothing else will satisfy. The psalmist wrote:

"As the deer pants for streams of water,
    so my soul pants for you, O God.
My soul thirsts for God, for the living God.
    When can I go and meet God?" (Ps 42:1-2)

I'm convinced that God is thrilled when we, like the psalmist, cry out to him and pursue him as the source of love and life. And I'm also convinced that God sometimes uses our greatest struggles to get our attention and show us how dependent we are on him.

Suffering and Failure Keep Our Vision Fresh

John Maxwell has written that we can "fail forward." Whenever we fail or fall, the act of getting up takes us one step farther down the road. We learn from our mistakes. These are hard lessons, but they are incredibly valuable. The willingness to risk assumes the willingness to experience failure.

If you are learning to ski, yet you avoid falling at all costs, you aren't pressing hard enough and you will never become a good skier. The fear of failure shackles your ability to learn. In the same way, boldness and strength in leadership promise great success, but never develop without some cost. Solomon wrote graphically of this principle, "Where there are no oxen, the manger is empty [of manure], but from the strength of the ox comes an abundant harvest" (Prov 14:4).

One of the times we are most vulnerable to the missiles and arrows of the evil one is after we have taken a risk and succeeded. When we are in the middle of the battle, we are usually much more aware of the attacks, the obstacles, and our dependence on God. The moment we have a victory, however, many of us let our guards down. It takes real maturity to remain dependent on God and aware of the attacks of the enemy even when we've experienced wonderful successes in ministry.

Suffering forces us to focus our hearts on the Lord and draw wisdom and strength from him. Paul's thorn in the flesh caused him great pain. He prayed three times for God to remove it, but God said "No." In Paul's suffering, the Lord spoke to him: "My grace is sufficient for you, for my power is made perfect in weakness" (II Cor 12:9). Paul realized that God's plan may require pain and suffering, but it is good and right. He chose to accept it as a part of God's gracious will for him to teach him humility and dependence.

Corrie ten Boom was no stranger to suffering, yet God gave her a wonderful perspective on his purpose during difficult times. She and her family were thrown into a Nazi concentration camp for hiding Jews during the German occupation. While in the prison, her sister Betsie died. Corrie commented:

"God has plans—not problems—for our lives. Before she died in the concentration camp in Ravensbruck, my sister Betsie said to me, 'Corrie, your whole life has been a training for the work you are doing here in prison—and for the work you will do afterward.'

"The life of a Christian is an education for higher service. No athlete complains when the training is hard. He thinks of the game, or the race. Looking back across the years of my life, I can see the working of a divine pattern which is the way of God with His children. When I was in a prison camp in Holland during the war, I often prayed, 'Lord, never let the enemy put me in a German concentration camp.' God answered no to that prayer. Yet in the German camp, with all its horror, I found many prisoners who had never heard of Jesus Christ.

"If God had not used my sister Betsie and me to bring them to Him, they would never have heard of Him. Many died, or were killed, but many died with the name of Jesus on their lips. They were well worth all our suffering. Faith is like radar which sees through the fog—the reality of things at a distance that the human eye cannot see."[25]

---

25 From "Portraits," In Touch Ministries, www.intouch.org/myintouch/
mighty/portraits/corrie_ten_boom

> *That's the way of the cross. We will do well to accept this fact so we won't be blindsided by difficulties.*

I want this to be an optimistic, upbeat, faith-filled book, but I don't want to give the impression that trusting God always leads to "broad sunlit plains" of success and happiness. Following the Father's will led Jesus to the cross. Following God led Paul into innumerable difficulties, rejection, and hardship. Following God leads us into mountaintops of joy and valleys of suffering. That's the way of the cross. We will do well to accept this fact so we won't be blindsided by difficulties.

In Paul's most joyful letter, he wrote the Philippians, "For it has been granted to you on behalf of Christ not only to believe on him, but also to suffer for him" (Phil 1:29). Suffering, Paul said, is a gift from God. Every time I take communion, I am reminded of what it cost God to invite me to have a relationship with him. My understanding of his great suffering for me gives me perspective on the little bit of suffering he has asked me to endure for him. Reflecting on this helps me stay on the cutting edge of gratitude and humility instead of demanding that God make my life easy and insisting that people respond positively to me.

When I forget the cost of suffering Christ paid for me, I lose the advantage I could gain from my own suffering. Pain is a great incentive (some would say, the greatest incentive) to change. C.S. Lewis called pain "God's megaphone" to get our attention, to call us to seek him with all our hearts, and to be willing to do whatever it takes to take another step toward him and his will.

Some of us have lived with lethargy and emptiness for a long, long time. We have rationalized our lack of passion for Christ and his kingdom, and we've become comfortable with our excuses. I hope that God uses this book to stir the fires again, to help such people take a hard look at his character and his calling so that we have a holy discontent with who we are and what we are doing. Then, and only then, will we have the motivation and tenacity to take the risks that bring real change.

Some of us suffer because we are willfully sinning. If that's the case, the remedy is obvious: repentance. Far more of us suffer because we expected great and glorious things to come from ministry, but it has been a lot harder work than we ever imagined. We have been ambushed by criticism, betrayal, and failure. One of the most important lessons we can learn is that life and ministry is hard. Unrealistic expectations of pain-free success always lead to bitter disappointment.

Paul encourages believers over and over again to endure, to have courage, and to develop tenacity in following the One who exemplifies both suffering and joy. The history of the expansion of the church is of men and women who suffered incredible hardships for the sake of Christ and his gospel. We should expect our experience to be no different. The strains in modern theology that promise "unfettered blessings if we just trust God" are deceptive and harmful. By promising too much, they destroy the hope they attempt to fulfill.

My own experience is that starting our church in Carson Valley has resulted in wonderful successes and terrific blessings. But many of these benefits have come at great cost to my family and me. I left a role with secure finances to dare to dream God's dream with a very unstable economic position. God has provided, sometimes miraculously, but there were times I wondered if I had asked my family to make too big a sacrifice.

When we moved here, my oldest daughter was about 13 years old. The church we attended in California had a vibrant youth ministry, but our fledgling little church here in Carson Valley didn't have one at all for a year and a half. Even now, our youth group has not grown into anything like the one she left five years ago. As a father, I have suffered the pangs of seeing my daughter not be challenged, not be stimulated, not experience the joys and fun of being a part of a large, exciting youth ministry. The Lord has used this time to deepen her faith and give her a maturity that perhaps she would not have gained if she had been in a bigger and better youth ministry, but that's the wisdom of hindsight. Other costs for the family have happened in the everyday realities of a new church "birthing" process that we never experienced in the established churches and denominational agency that I had served before.

Following Christ exacts a personal price, like the one my family has experienced during the last five years, as well as an organizational price. God's vision for an organization is the upheaval that comes with change. As I have talked to hundreds of pastors at conferences over the years, many respond very positively at first to the call to a fresh, God-given vision for their churches. As the series of meetings continue, however, I notice the fire of excitement fade on many of their faces. They begin to realize what change means, not only for them, but also for their leaders, their members, and a few curmudgeons who would fight them every step of the way. They simply aren't willing to pay that price.

One pastor told me sadly, "I'm just not willing to do what it takes to move forward. Now that I see what you're talking about, I think it would cause more problems than it would solve." I was incredulous. All I was asking them to do was to respond in faith and boldness to Christ's Great Commandment and Great Commission. My message shouldn't have been new to them. It shouldn't have been radical in the least. It is the stuff of faith, life, and ministry—

especially for those who say they've been called by God to reach the world and shepherd God's flock.

Keep the Vision Fresh by Passing It On

A vision that is contained dies. A vision that is shared grows stronger and sharper. Each of us has been entrusted with a vision, a calling to be a part of God's divine will. If we aren't thrilled that we have been chosen and adopted by the King of the universe and given a role as his ambassador to a lost and dying world, we need to have an EKG!

> *If we aren't thrilled that we have been chosen and adopted by the King of the universe and given a role as his ambassador to a lost and dying world, we need to have an EKG!*

As a leader, my role is to pass my God-given vision along to every person around me. From the associate pastor to any visitor at one of our outreaches, I want each person to grasp the incredible privilege of being God's and being used by God. Every time I see a person's eyes light up with newfound faith, the vision becomes even stronger and clearer in my own heart, and I know the vision will spread because that person can't wait to tell someone else about the treasure of meaning and love he has found.

My task is to tailor my communication of the vision for different audiences so they can understand and accept it. To leaders, I share a lot of background information and perspectives because they are moved by an ever deeper, ever growing grasp of that vision. We talk about many of the principles I've included in this book, and we discuss how they apply to each situation and each person in our church. At our worship services, I focus on the primary essentials of our core values and the motivation of the love of God. I gladly and unapologetically invite every person to respond to that vision by getting involved in a meaningful way. And even at our outreach events, I tell people that we are happy they have come, and we hope they will find grace and joy in knowing Christ. That discovery will be the doorway to a larger vision for each person.

Another aspect of passing the vision along is a willingness to train others who are so skilled and effective that we run the risk of their taking our places. I ask our leaders, and especially our staff, if they are willing to recruit and train someone who might prove to be better at their roles than they are. I ask myself the same question to keep my motives in check. I hope I would be thrilled to pour my life into someone in such a way that he becomes such a good leader and speaker that our church says, "We'd rather have him."

Barnabas was a leader in the early church, but when Paul came along, Barnabas was willing to acknowledge Paul's unmistakable gifts and take a backseat to the new guy on the block. As a result of his humility, the mission of the church was propelled into greater effectiveness.

Corrie ten Boom said, "I will not grasp anything from God. I will live my life with open palms. God has placed many things under my care, and I will allow him to remove anything he chooses to remove." Are we clutching our roles, our positions of authority and respect, our salaries, or safety with clinched fists? Or do we hold these things with open hands, acknowledging they are gifts from God that he can take away anytime he wants?

One of my favorite paintings is of a young man at the wheel of a ship on the ocean. Christ stands behind him with one hand on the man's shoulder and the other pointing the way to the future through the stormy seas. A couple of things stand out to me. First, Christ's hand is not on the wheel. He gives that responsibility to the young man. How many times does God direct us toward an uncertain future when we'd rather keep sailing in calm water? And second, Christ is right there with the young man pointing the way and encouraging him. When God calls us, the seas may be stormy and we may be afraid, but he is always beside us. If we pay attention to him, he can give us the courage and direction we need to make it through. After making it through a storm or two, the young man will have enough knowledge of God's direction and care to pass his experience on to others. But his wisdom and courage are not honed in the harbor, but in the open, stormy sea.

When we were planning the launch of our church, I wasn't worried about the first year. I was concerned about the second year. I knew by then we would have a lot of young Christians crying out for attention. It would be easy to become absorbed in their needs and allow the clarity and balance of our calling to be eroded. My concerns proved to be valid. By the second year, I had far more demands on my time and energies than I could handle.

At that time, the Lord confirmed a very important principle: Young Christians grow best in the context of a powerful blend of outreach and nurture. It is a mistake, for many reasons, to focus their attention only on their own growth. They grow far more if they are involved in consistently taking the gospel to those who still need the saving touch of the Master. Their involvement in outreach reminds them of the grace of God, causes them to depend on God to work through them, and builds strong relationships as they work with others to reach the community. And young believers are often the most enthusiastic about their faith because it so fresh, rich, and real to them.

Outreach should not be tacked on as an afterthought. It is the heartbeat of God "to seek and to save the lost." Taking the gospel to unbelievers, not waiting for them to come to us, is a primary mission of the church. It is also a primary prod to the faith of believers. We never think of adding a discussion of outreach to our planning because it is central to our planning. The questions in our discussions revolve around the details of when, where, how, and who to involve in the activities.

A New Measuring Stick

Certainly, numbers are a significant measure of growth, but I believe another one is much richer: changed lives. This measuring stick doesn't produce guilt, and it doesn't thrive on comparison.

In my years of being a pastor and a denominational executive, I've seen that most Christian leaders have a single measurement that defines success: the number of people involved. Certainly, numbers are a significant measure of growth, but I believe another one is much richer: changed lives. This measuring stick doesn't produce guilt, and it doesn't thrive on comparison. Instead of wondering if our church is bigger or is growing faster than someone else's church, I focus on, I pray for, I eagerly anticipate God working in such a powerful way that people's lives are changed for eternity. I look for unbelievers to turn to Christ for forgiveness and purpose, and I look for believers to respond to God's incredible greatness and grace and say, "Lord, here I am. I'm yours, and I'm eager to follow you." That's what rings my bell!

Changed lives must have been the measuring stick for Paul, too. He wrote the believers in Thessalonica: "For what is our hope, our joy, or the crown in which we will glory in the presence of our Lord Jesus when he comes? Is it not you? Indeed, you are our glory and joy" (I Thess 2:19-20).

The desire to avoid risks and to be safe in existing organizational structures stimulates all that is bad in church leadership. It produces fear and comparison, guilt and drivenness, using people instead of loving them, and discouragement instead of enthusiasm. Real ministry with real people isn't safe. It's messy. It can be chaotic, and in fact, the movement of God's Spirit is uncontrolled (by us, at least).

If I were to compare our church to any New Testament church, I would compare it to Corinth. Our people have many of the same struggles. Paul didn't try to control them by pointing them to rigid organizational structures. He pointed them to the matchless Savior. He reminded them of the benefits of following Christ, and he warned them of the consequences of disobedience. He told them Christ is their greatest treasure. Structures don't touch hearts or change lives. Christ does.

Paul said we have the treasure of the gospel in earthen vessels, in jars of clay, in cracked pots. We have no right to assume that God would love us and give us the incredible privilege of partnership with him. It is a gift, an unspeakable wonder, that the God of heaven and earth has chosen flawed and failing cracked pots to transport his heavenly treasure and leak his grace onto others. That's why I get up every day with a sense of excitement. When I see the love of God touch a person and I see that life changed, restored and refreshed, I am thrilled that God is willing to use me in some small way in that eternal transaction. To be at that place at that time with a heart full of thankfulness to God has cost me something, but that, for me at least, is well worth the risk.

Reflection

1. Read I Thessalonians 1 and 2. Jot down your observations of how someone as busy and responsible as Paul could keep his calling so fresh.

2. Read Revelation 1:9-18. How does this passage speak to you about the awesome wonder of the greatness of Christ?

    Are you overwhelmed more by your stresses or by God's awesome greatness today? Explain.

3. Suffering and failure can either devastate or strengthen a person. What are some factors that determine which will be the ultimate outcome for an individual?

4. What are some ways "passing it on" helps keep a vision fresh?

5. What is the next step for you as you think and pray about applying the principles and strategies in this book?

Kingdom Ventures:
Your Church Development Company

PRODUCTS

Kingdom Ventures is committed to helping churches and their people grow. Carson Valley Christian Center (mentioned in this book) has used many of Kingdom Ventures' products, including their Gifts & Apparel division (iExaltmall.com, Sierra Candles, Yahwear and Mr. Roy Productions), their Technology & Partnership efforts (Xtreme Notebooks, Bible Software, and Affiliate Relationships) and their Media & Marketing Properties (iExalt.com and Christian Times).

SERVICES

Kingdom Ventures has a full range of services, including church financing, filtered internet services, online fundraising programs, product-driven fundraising programs, and a host of additional services that will equip your church for growth. In addition, Kingdom Ventures also hosts iExalt.com, a leading Christian portal for the Internet with the largest evangelical search directory on the world wide web.

CHRISTIAN TIMES.

For additional information, visit us at
www.kdmvcorp.com or at
www.iexalt.com

If you'd like to do your online shopping with us, visit **www.iexaltmall.com**

You may also call us at **800.839.2506**
or e-mail us at **info@kdmvcorp.com**

VisionQuest Ministries:
Forging Leadership Pathways
for the Future

Dr. John Jackson has a number of additional resources to equip you and your church in areas of leadership, church growth, and teaching.

Some of our many resources include the following:

- Audio Teaching Tapes
- Helpful Leadership Articles
- Worship Resources
- Celebration Arts Scripts

These are available at VisionQuest Ministries on the Internet at

www.vqresources.com

High Impact Church Planting

You'll be particularly interested in *High Impact Church Planting,* the book that describes how Carson Valley Christian Center was successfully launched past the 200 barrier, and grew past the 1,000 barrier in only three years. Today, after just 5 years of ministry life, there are over 1,500 people in worship each weekend at Carson Valley Christian Center (www.carsonvalleychristian.com). This growth took place in a community with fewer than 100,000 people within 30 miles and where less than 5% of the people attend church on a given weekend. To order copies of *High Impact Church Planting,* visit us online at **www.vqresources.com** or call us at **775.267.2242**.

Dr. Jackson Is Available to Help You and Your Ministry

If you are interested in having Dr. Jackson speak at your conference, provide personal mentoring and coaching, or consulting with your church or ministry organization, contact him at **john@carsonvalleychristian.com**

For more copies of PastorPreneur . . .

I encourage you to use this book as a foundation for rich, stimulating discussions with your church leadership team. Get a copy for each person, and ask them to read a chapter or two and answer the questions at the end of the chapters before you meet.

Many leadership teams discuss a chapter of *PastorPreneur* at a time, but you may want to tackle several chapters on a leadership retreat. However you choose to use this material, trust God to deepen people's grasp of God's greatness and his desire to use every person in the church in the greatest adventure the world has ever known!

D I S C O U N T S
2–6 books . . . .$18.50 each
7–12 books . . . .$17.50 each
Over 12 books . . . .$16.00 each

Shipping . . . .$1 per book
However, if you order over 10 books, we will ship for FREE!

O R D E R   I N F O R M A T I O N
Books (#): _____ books at _____ = _____
Shipping: _____ books at _____ = _____
Total: _____

Call: **775.267.2242** to order
Email: **bookorder@kdmvcorp.com**
Write: **Kingdom Ventures,** 1045 Stephanie Way, Minden, NV 89423
Internet: **www.iexaltmall.com**

Checks or Credit Cards accepted by phone at 775.267.2242.